RavenWind

Hartzell Cobbs

Interior Image Credit: Rick Bartow

The Richard E. Bartow Irrevocable Trust, The Richard E. Bartow Testamentary Trusts, and Froelick Gallery licenses non-exclusive reproduction privileges to Hartzell Cobbs for four (4) artworks by Rick Bartow:
"Man in the Box XII," 1987, pastel, graphite on paper, 40x26"
"Absinthe Dream," 2008, handcolored drypoint, 11x8" image, published by Moon Dog Press, Newport, OR, / Tokyo.
"Blue Raven Bundle," 2001/2005, lithography, edition of 20, 42.5x30.5", published by Brodsky Center at Rutgers University, NJ.
"Red Raven Bundle," 2001/2005, lithograph, edition of 20, 42.5x30.5", published by Brodsky Center at Rutgers University, NJ.
All copyrights to the art are retained by The Richard E. Bartow Irrevocable Trust. Artwork courtesy of Froelick Gallery, Portland, OR.

"The Jon Turk Story," courtesy of author, Jon Turk.

Archway Publishing books may be ordered through booksellers or by contacting:

Archway Publishing
1663 Liberty Drive
Bloomington, IN 47403
www.archwaypublishing.com
1 (888) 242-5904

ISBN: 978-1-4808-7375-9 (sc)
ISBN: 978-1-4808-7374-2 (e)

Library of Congress Control Number: 2019930773

Print information available on the last page.

Archway Publishing rev. date: 01/29/2019

ARCHWAY PUBLISHING

To Joy in my life

TABLE OF CONTENTS

ETERNAL RAVEN

RavenWind

From legend I was born
Creator of the visible world
steeped in primordial darkness
providing
water in drought
salmon in famine
I am movement upon the wind
the spirit between two worlds.
Of opposites am I made.
Wings soaring
in the darkness and the light
the known and mysterious
the worldly and unseen.
Both flesh and spirit are my gifts
guiding the brave in battle
with vision from the otherworld

I am the without and within
challenging you to face the
shadow of yourself.
Fears with power to destroy
hopes with strength to create.
In both I reside.
Of these am I
spirit, flesh,
with enlightenment to give.
Within the mundane and the finite
you, as I, will find the gift of immortality
I am Raven in the Wind.

Wings on the Wind

Wind blows, fog lifts, a distant caw
from the world of SpiritWind, Dark Brother comes
ever present, yet oft unseen.
The winged one brings
truth of ourselves
binding us to this world and the Other.

The Other, the Great Spirit
within all, yet bigger than the universe
smaller than the atom
yet smaller still.

Creator and Destroyer Breath,
Great Mystery upon Wind
Spirit Raven soars.
From one world into the next
And back again.

INTRODUCTION: FOLKLORE THROUGH THE AGES

Raven's story is best told where the great bird often resides, in folklore.

The term "folk" emerged in the eighteenth century as industrialization separated people from the natural world. With this separation came the feeling that something pure and spiritual was being lost. "Folk" refers to two or more people. We can't be "folk" by ourselves. We are "folk" when there are at least two of us. "Folk" was any subgroup of the general populations that operated with its own expressions, words, tradition and history, giving the group an identity unto itself.

"Lore" is the tradition and body of knowledge on a subject that is held by a particular group and is passed on from generation to generation. "Lore" takes many forms such as art or story that embodies the tradition of a group and is passed down over time by members of the group. It can be contemporary, ancient, or anywhere in between.

The word "folklore" was coined in 1846 by the English scholar, William John Thoms. The word categorizes the Brothers Grimm stories told from 1812-1852 and gathered into one collection by the brothers. The Grimm tales connected Germans to a common cultural past that defined them in ways wars won and lost could not.

The industrial revolution in Europe and in America was threatening the quality and historical definition of people's lives. Folklore uplifted the relevance of daily living expressed through words and art that were being lost by the impingement of modern life. Group identity, history, and meaning were preserved through folklore.

The great folklorist, Alan Dundes, in his book, <u>Meaning of Folklore,</u> argues effectively that written or verbalized folklore is much more than a didactic story; it is a story with symbolism encouraging the receiver of the folklore to provide her own interpretation.

Dundes views folklore as an artistic process that is continually reinterpreted and/or newly created and shared by a group of two or more.

In his charming book, <u>Never Try to Teach a Pig to Sing</u>, Dundes demonstrates that social media is a major conduit for folklore. He provides countless examples of contemporary humor as folklore that is particularly suited to social media.

Folklore gives societal subgroups identity, creates community, and provides an outlet for all types of art. We understand ourselves better and find rapport with others when we share family stories, inside jokes with friends, or appreciate the artwork of a group making Christmas ornaments for a church sale.

One of my most prized possessions is a quilt made from discarded clothing by a group of elderly women I knew well. I feel at one with them and our shared heritage whenever I take the time to look at their beautiful handiwork. It is folk art that will be passed down to my grandchildren and hopefully beyond.

Folklore comes to life when it provides personal roots for our self-identity and gives us rapport with others in our "community." Folklore can help us identify with people we know, the memory of folks who have died, or with people we don't know but with whom we share something in common, or a combination of the three.

Folklore is often 'hidden in plain sight." It can be stories shared around the kitchen table, over a campfire, or from the pulpit. It can be folk songs, rock, bluegrass, hip hop, or a Lakota flutist rendering anew an ancient courtship song. Folklore can be a painting or a quilt that opens our mind and our thoughts and gives expression in the moment while tying us to our ancestral past. Folklore gives us a "place," a context, an understanding of where we came from, who we are, and where we are headed.

Folklore takes on a multitude of interpretations and meanings depending on the life, history, and current environment of an individual or group. While it may have deep historical roots, it always relates to the present in one way or another. The process of placing tradition in conversation with one's current situation and finding insight and guidance is called "hermeneutics." Folklore allows us to hermeneutically take an old story and apply it to our current situation.

An interpretation of folklore at one point in life may differ from the interpretation at another time. With every interpretation comes a reminder of the continuing need to rekindle our energy for daily living, to keep in touch with our inner life force, and avoid apathy and coldness in ourselves and towards others. This book will reference white ravens turning black. In today's world this could be viewed as racist, however, no such interpretation is appropriate. The stories give a reason as to why raven is black, or there is a blending of white and black raven into one, reminiscent of the Yin and Yang in Chinese philosophy that shows how contradictory forces can be complimentary.

Stagnancy of thought and rigidity of belief make us boring. Folklore challenges us to relate our inner life force to our ever changing lives.

It is the dynamics of creative openness and "seeing all things new" that brings excitement and meaning to our lives. Our personal interpretations inform ourselves and communities, as the interpretation of others informs us.

Specific cultures also play a role in interpreting folklore. For example, a group of people living in a city may consider a raven as just part of the environment and tell stories about how the bird acts. But to the Northwest Native American steeped in folklore and a mythological worldview, the Raven draws a person or group into a space vibrating with life and filled with magic. Raven is a magical being in Northwest Native American folklore, while it may be only a nuisance in downtown Baltimore. The rich Raven folklore of Native Americans may seem ridiculous, irrelevant, and even primitive to the city slicker.

Folklore speaks about the world and all forms of life that reside there. In written folklore, the reader will encounter time and again stories of creation, destruction, the spiritual world, powerful heroes, and tricksters.

When the spoken word is the medium for folklore, there are three basic genres: 1) **Folktales** that are fictional. Such stories may or may not have any symbolic meaning. They may have a moral point or be told only for amusement. Such tales begin with words such as "Once upon a time…". The tales are often directed to children and filled with humor. 2) **Legends** are told as literally true but generally not believed literally. They are set in the real world, not a fictional one. They are more of a commentary on contemporary life and related to things we are stressed about. Legends begin with phrases such as "Raven was flying over the lake when…" or "Raven was hungry, but he was lazy…." The events in legends are told as if they have just happened. 3) **Myths** are told as sacred truth, but are not dependent on literal truth. Myths are set in the literal world, and generally in ancient times or the time of creation. They use mediums between the spiritual and physical worlds. Myths teach us how the world, animals, humans, and all things were created and how everything has its place. Myths inform and define the world's religions even when they are understood to be based in something that is literally untrue or superstitious. They explain why life is as it is.[1]

"Urban myths" are technically more like legends. They are stories that didn't really happen, have a contemporary setting, and an amazing staying power. Examples of such "myths" (or legends) coming from the recent past but not literally true are stories of alligators in New York sewers, the moon landing being faked, and the other meaning of the movie "Frozen" being that Walt Disney's body was cryogenically frozen (he was actually cremated in 1966).

Myths, legends, and folktales tell their stories with authors generally unknown. Contemporary Native American folklore, when expressed through folk art or stories, may or may not reveal the artist.

It is through myths and legends continually retold that everything important for Native American life is found: creation of the world, sun, and moon, the color of the mountains, the four directions, the spirit life of trees, and the rich lore specific to each animal and bird. All this is central to the social structure, values, spiritual realities, and daily life of the Native American.

Wherever raven families are found, which is in most parts of the world, they are usually presented in local folklore as highly intelligent ancient messengers of the gods, although occasionally they are buffoons. This bird who developed its current brain power some eight million years ago is the earth's smartest bird and one of the smartest animals, along with chimpanzees and dolphins. As such, Raven is central to mythology worldwide.

[1] Summarized from Folklore Rules: A Fun, Quick, and Useful Introduction, by Lynne S. McNeill, Utah State University Press, p. 40.

Raven of folklore calls us to follow, to listen, and experience life in all its complexity, insight, ambiguity, contradiction, and humor. You are invited to join me as we look at Raven in world history and in Native American myths, legends and folktales.

Feel the presence of the spiritual in the mundane,
discover anew things we know but cannot explain,
quiver inside at the experience of magic,
recognize the paradoxes within the world and ourselves,
respect the sciences and know there is more,
and feel the unseen winds breathing the spirit of life into us.

CHAPTER ONE: WORLDWIDE RAVEN FOLKLORE

"You don't believe that Raven created the world?"

"I don't know. I suppose. It's what I was taught. But I've always wondered about the other religions. The Christian god is supposed to have created the world in seven days."

"Their world—not ours."

"I don't understand."

"Here in the dreamlands, all times and all possibilities exist at once, and some of them are reflected in the first world. Now, can we keep driving?"[2]

THE INTERNATIONAL RAVEN

Ravens have appeared in lore dating to earliest years of recorded history, sometimes as omens of bad tidings or destroyers of what is. At other times the raven is the messenger of the gods, a bridge between the material and spiritual, or even entrusted by the Great Spirit to create the world and give it life. There is no evidence that Raven was ever worshipped, rather he is the bearer of magic, and a harbinger of messages from the cosmos. Such messages come from beyond time and space.

Intermingled with Creator/Destroyer is Raven acting selfish, deceptive, or cunning to quench his never ending appetite, mainly for food. A trickster he is.

Much of Europe saw ravens as personifications of evil. In France, people believed ravens were the souls of wicked priests (crows were wicked nuns). In Germany, ravens were the incarnations of damned souls, even the devil himself. In Sweden, ravens that cawed at night were the souls of murdered people who didn't have a proper Christian burial. In Denmark, people believed that night ravens were exorcised spirits of evil people. They believed night ravens had a hole in their left wing created by the stake that had bound them to the ground. In Danish folksongs and many other cultures, ravens consume the bodies of the dead on the battlefield. Also, if a raven ate the heart of a fallen king he gained the king's knowledge and could perform magic. In Scotland, Banshees could take the shape of ravens and act as an omen of death to the households they flew over.

[2] The Wind in His Heart by Charles de Lint, Triskel Press, Ottaway, ON, Canada. p. 217.

In another part of the world, Indian Hinduism has Brahma, the creator god, appearing as a raven in one of his incarnations. The other two major gods in the Hindu triad are Vishnu, who sustains the world, and Shiva, who is the god of destruction. Hinduism balances the creator Brahma with the destroyer Shiva and places Vishnu between them, acting as a balancer and keeping the opposites working together. When the opposites are recognized and accepted in life, balanced results and wisdom come.

These three gods are joined by one of the most important and popular gods in Hindu mythology, the son of Shiva, Ganesha. He has an elephant head and a human body. He represents the soul (atman) and the physical (maya). Genesha is also the Trickster in Hindu mythology. Stories of his tricks abound and with them his ability to make people laugh. He is kind, generous, humorous, and understands human nature. He acquired his elephant head when Vishnu cut off his original head and Genesha's mother replaced it with the only head available, an elephant's. Genesha rides around on a rat.

Behind all the gods is Atman, a word that in Sanskrit means "breath." Atman is eternal, imperishable, beyond time and space. He is not of body or mind or consciousness but is something beyond them. He is Spirit. Atman makes all things function and is the source of all the workings in the universe. Vayu, the god of wind, is rooted in the Atman. Vayu is the movement of Atman.

Historically, one of the earliest cave paintings (20,000 years old) at Lascaux in southwestern France tells the story of a Raven priest. Lascaux is supplemented by many Paleolithic or Stone Age (approximately 3 million years ago to 12,000 BC) paintings and cave inscriptions around the world telling of Raven shamans, their births, victories, deaths and the final transformation from human to raven form.

In Greek mythology Coronis is the crow or raven deity that brings rain to protect the grain harvest. Coronis is associated with death as the ruler of the underworld known as Elysium.

The goddess Coronis, one of the seven sisters of light who are rain-makers, is the parent, along with Apollo, of the great healing god Asclepius. Coronis cheats on Apollo, who finds out and has Coronis killed. Apollo's raven did not stop Coronis's infidelity, and Apollo punishes the raven by changing his color from white to black.

Folklore even ties Alexander the Great to ravens. When Alexander was lost in the desert west of Egypt, two ravens appeared and guided him to safety at the oasis of Siwa.

In Celtic mythology, dating back to the Iron Age (approximately 1200—700 BC), the warrior goddess known as *Morrighan*, often appears in the form of a raven. In some Welsh tales the raven, called *Mobinogion*, is the harbinger of death. Many witch tales through the centuries allow them to transform into ravens and fly away, evading otherwise inevitable capture and possible death. The raven, mentioned in ancient text such as '*The Tain*' in Ireland and the Anglo Saxon classic '*Beowul*', perches with confidence and surveys his terrain.

In the Hebrew Talmud, ravens teach mankind how to deal with death. When Cain slew Abel, a raven showed Adam and Eve how to bury the body, because they had never done it before. In the Bible ravens may have a special intimacy with God as his messenger, for example, feeding a holy hermit during a time of turmoil and drought. “And the ravens brought him bread and meat in the morning, and bread and meat in the evening; and he drank from the brook” (I Kings 17:6). The magical ability of the raven is not questioned.

There are countless examples of ravens appearing in Christian art. St. Oswald holds a raven with a ring in his mouth and St. Benedict has a raven at his feet. Saint Paul the Hermit appears in art with a raven bringing him a loaf of bread. In contradictory Christian traditions, ravens represent the solitude of the holy hermits as well as the souls of wicked priests and witches. As already mentioned, in the history of myth, legend, and folktale contradictions abound.

A wonderful Raven myth comes from Norse mythology. Norse mythology is a body of myths from the North Germanic people with written records from the second century BC and extending into late antiquity (sixth century AD). The oral origin of Odin goes back to the sixth century BC.

Norse mythology boasts of the god Odin, one of its most complex characters and Father of all the Gods and men. He is the unifying factor behind all the characteristics associated with living: war, sovereignty, wisdom, magic, shamanism, poetry, and the dead. Odin went through a ritual of death and rebirth in order to acquire his powers. Such an experience is a prerequisite to becoming a shaman in most every culture. He was big and hairy and had only one eye that functioned. Many stories say his empty eye socket was sacrificed for wisdom. His wife is the goddess Frigg who is famous for her wisdom and foreknowledge.

Two ravens accompanied Odin—one on each shoulder. In some stories there was initially one raven, but, with the passage of time, fate split the bird, and then there were two. One of the ravens was named Huginn (“Thought”) and the other Muninn (“Memory”). One holds all memory and the other lives with only that day’s thoughts in mind.

At the crack of dawn Huginn and Muninn would fly out across the Norse world to return in the evening (some stories say they returned after breakfast) with knowledge of what they had seen and learned that day. No physical characteristics made the ravens stand out. They could travel the world incognito. Flying across the Norse world in a day meant they had to travel magically fast. Time and distance would not allow for a normal raven to make such a trip.

Out of Norse folklore, came the following anonymous poem:

Raven's black
On wings of night.
Nine worlds circle
In their flight.

One-eyed Father
Hears their call.
Tidings brought
To Asgard's hall.

Thought as fast
As lighting's flash.
Mem'ry old
As sacred Ash.

Huginn, Muninn
See and hear.
Whispers all

In some versions of the Odin myth the two ravens become part of Odin's own consciousness. In all the stories Huginn and Muninn were central to Odin's power. Their role was to serve as advisors to Odin on how to approach opposing forces in battle. Having the ability to speak, a common trait of animals in folklore, they can talk to Odin.

As messengers they kept him informed about the activities in his kingdom and maintained his outstanding memory. Coming from the Spirit World, where their flight was not bound by time, their ability to speak and communicate with Odin came naturally and allowed the mythical Odin to reside in both the material and spiritual worlds.

There are many tales and legends telling how ravens arrived at the Tower of London and why they remain to this day. One of the more interesting legends comes from the Welsh.

In Britain, the giant Bran is the mythical King in Welsh mythology, well known in the Iron Age of Britain (800 BC-43 AD). The name "Bran" means "Holy Raven," and the ravens were messengers between the mortal world and the spirits of the Otherworld.

In a Welsh legend, originating in the twelfth century, Bran was mortally wounded while fighting the Irish. He commanded his warriors to behead him and take his head to the Tower of London where it was to be buried as a sign that he would protect Britain. Black ravens became the symbol of Bran and reveal his sacred spirit. Out of this story folklore arose declaring that if the ravens ever left the Tower of London, the monarchy would fall. To this day the ravens are cared for and protected at the Tower of London.

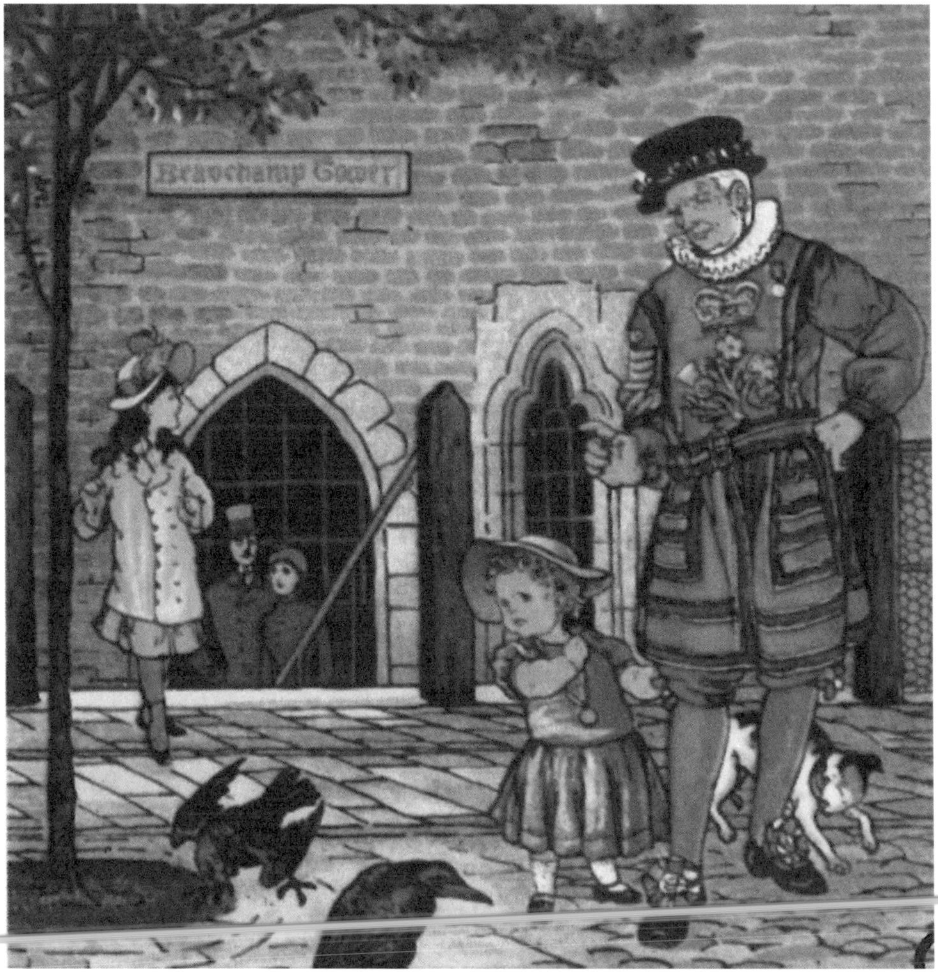

From the children's book London Tower (1883), artwork by Ellen Houghton (1853-1922) and Thomas Crane (1843-1903).

Humor also played a role in raven folklore throughout the world. One such folktale, several hundred years old, came out of Iceland:

A long married couple found a raven chick. They took the small bird home and cared for it. One day a visitor came by and asked why they were giving so much attention to the bird that could easily live on its own. The old couple told him: “We have heard that ravens can live for three hundred years. We are going to keep it to see if it is true.”

SIBERIAN RAVEN

There is another part of the world where Raven folklore goes back for thousands of years. The first Americans entered the North American continent about 20,000 years ago, crossing from Siberia over the Bering land bridge during the last ice age. Within the groups traveling over the ice were the shamans of Siberia accompanied by their drums, rattles, flutes and the mythical raven.

Shamans often used Raven as his or her mediator to the Great Spirit. The Siberian Raven endowed with magical powers, can be brave and cunning one moment and greedy and gluttonous the next. He brings to humans the gifts of fire, light, and food. Then again, he can wreak havoc on just about everything. His gluttony leads him on a never-ending quest for food, securing it through any trickery or deception necessary.

Kutkh is the most common name given to the revered Raven Spirit of the Russian Far East. *Kutkh* appears in many myths and legends as a key figure in creation, as a fertile ancestor of mankind, as a mighty shaman, and as a trickster. He is a popular subject of the animal stories of the Chukchi people of Siberia and plays a central role in the mythology of the Koryaks and the Itelmens of Karnchatka.

There are many legends where *Kutkh* has interaction and uses trickery with other animal spirits. At times *Kutkh* will come out on top and in other stories be made a fool.

In one Chukchi myth *Kutkh,* the mighty raven, is flying with the wind through the cosmos. Tired from constant flight, he regurgitates the earth from his gut, turns himself into an old man, and lands on the flat empty land to rest. As Raven takes his first steps on land, mice emerge. The mice are curious, playful, and fearless. *Ktukh* becomes tired of walking, falls asleep, and the mice enter his nose. This causes Raven to sneeze mightily, buckling the earth and resulting in the creation of mountains and valleys. As the great bird attempts to stamp out the mountains, he ends up forming the oceans. Further harassments by the mice lead to great a battle between snow and fire, which creates the seasons. Hence, the world as people know it was created through interaction of the mighty *Kutkh* and many thousands of small mice.

NATIVE AMERICAN RAVEN

It is understandable that many of the ancient stories in Siberia regarding *Kutkh* are much like those told in the Pacific Northwest. For example, the bringing of light in the form of the sun and the moon is a common theme. Sometimes *kutkh* tricks an evil spirit which has captured the celestial bodies, much like some of the Raven myths and legends the from Tlingit and Haida tribes in the upper Pacific Northwest. In other Northwest stories, it is Raven who must be tricked into releasing the sun and the moon from his bill as he flies over the earth. From Sitka, Alaska, comes the myth of Raven dropping water he has stolen from his beak. The dropped water turns into the lakes, rivers, and streams of Alaska.

Both Siberian and Northwest Native American folklore endow Raven with magical powers. The magical bird can be brave and cunning one moment and greedy and gluttonous the next. In the Northwest, as in Siberia, Raven brings to humans the gifts of fire, light, and food. His gluttony leads him on a never-ending quest for food, securing it through any means necessary.

Here I sit, countless centuries after the arrival of Raven mythology to the Northwest, relaxed and sipping early morning coffee from my well-worn mug, looking out over the Payette Lake from the deck of a small mountain place, in McCall, Idaho, I call home. The fog envelops the lake as my eyes wander across its partially fog hidden waters, bringing me the familiar feeling of mystery and magic that has drawn me to this place since childhood.

Out of the silently lifting fog the lake is coming to life and I hear the ancient cry, "Caw," followed by the mythical bird sweeping downward, flaunting its near four foot wingspan, and gracefully landing atop a nearby Tamarack.

Hearing the call of the raven I am reminded its voice is fuller, the wing span longer, and the beak more angled than that of its closest corvid family member, the crow. These differences are irrelevant in folklore where the two birds are generally interchangeable.

The raven usually travels in pairs or in family units. The raven is considered one of the smartest animals, right up there with chimpanzees and dolphins, and is the smartest bird on the planet. This great bird can live up to twenty years in the wild and forty in captivity. In mythology Raven is eternal.

Ravens drop rocks on people to keep them from climbing a tree to reach his nest. He will steal fish by pulling the line of an ice fisherman out of the ice hole and eating the fish while the fisherman sleeps. The raven pretends to hide food in one place while hiding it in another to keep fellow ravens from finding and eating it before him.

It is this bird that calls to me as it has others for countless generations before me.

As the silky black of the raven's coat with a tinge of white shines subtly through the grayness of the morning, time is lost and my mind moves deeper into the myths and legends that accompany the bird who cocks his head to the left as if listening to an anthem I cannot hear but sense.

It is early May 2018. I am on the deck of my place overlooking Payette Lake in McCall, Idaho, where I am beckoned to enter the world of beauty, humor, myth, legend, magic, and power; a world where Raven has the ability to not just communicate but speak with humans. In fact, Raven is a shape-shifter, meaning he can take on the physical form of other objects or beings, including humans, and can communicate with the spoken word.

The Raven of myth and legend is alive and well in my soul.

Payette Lake is a 5,330 acre expanse, filled with clean, snow-melt water, resting in the Payette National Forest at 5,000 feet. It was carved some 10,000 years ago by a glacier 1,000 feet high, 2.5 miles in width and 8 miles long. The lake reaches a depth of over 300 feet. The first inhabitants of the land around the lake were the Tukudeka, a sub-band of the Shoshone known as the 'Sheepeaters." Between one and four thousand years ago these early ancestors of the Shoshone lived a rhythmic life with the cyclical four seasons around the lake. The land was sacred, dwelt and celebrated upon in the summers, and migrated away from in the harsh winters. Raven shared the land with them. Native American Raven stories are prevalent in the Northwest, from Central California through Alaska, and extending eastward to encompass Idaho's Payette Lake. Raven stories appear among the Athabaskan speaking peoples of Canada and Alaska. While tribes such as the Sioux have some Raven tales, they use the Spotted Eagle and the buffalo, indigenous to the Central Plains area, to perform many of the same functions as Raven in the Northwest.

Raven stories vary among the tribes even though the stories may use the same titles. However, there are certain attributes Raven possesses that remain consistent regardless of the tribe. Raven is always a magical figure and able to take any form he desires. His personal needs always trump any altruistic tendency he may have. And this strange creator of the world has built loss and destruction into nature. In one story from the Sioux, Raven makes man from clay. Man is angry and wonders why Raven didn't make them out of rock so they wouldn't die. Raven does not answer.

In the world of myth there is only one Raven who is the Creator/Destroyer/Trickster, but no one knows which raven it is. In folklore Raven has specific hardwired characteristics; however, the interpretation of the stories about Raven myths and legends requires our personal participation and willingness to be open to Raven's insights and apply them to ourselves.

The magical and mythical sides of Raven are characterized in the poem RavenWind, found at the beginning of this book, and manifested in the many and oft told creation stories. As we have already seen, his creative/

destructive powers are supplemented by his Trickster traits. Raven can be the bravest hero and the most deceitful and cunning of birds.

The morning sun is casting a shadow from the great Tamaracks on the now pristine-still waters of the long ago glacier created lake. The fog has lifted. The cawing of the raven who is coming and going from his perch on the tall Tamarack tree draws me into his world of beauty and myth—a world where all in creation, animals, trees, and even rocks, share the same spirit. It is a mythical world where Raven brought life into all that is and placed the Sun in the heavens to complement the darkness. He dwells in a world not bound by the materialistic, non-mythical view of reality that is so prevalent in today's world. Raven draws me to ancient tradition and folklore. I am home.

Stories told and written for millennium have shown how humans love, respect, and fear Raven's power. Humans since times long forgotten have laughed at his tricks, admired his strength, and in sacred moments allowed Raven to guide. Shamans have enlisted Raven's help in making people well or guiding them to the Other World. The Raven rattle is often used in conjunction with drumming by the shaman to enter the Spirit World.

BLACK AND WHITE RAVEN

The mythical character of Raven is exemplified in the enduring and much told folklore on how Raven became black.

The myths and legends of ravens changing colors are found in many traditions. For example, in the popular Old Testament story of the Great flood, when it stops raining Noah sends out a white raven to find dry land. He does not return, so Noah sends out a white dove who returns with an olive branch in his beak showing that there is indeed dry land. In the Jewish Talmud the raven was punished for not returning by being turned black and forced to feed on carrion from that day forward.

The theme of how ravens got their black feathers is prevalent in Native American Folklore.

There is an Alaskan story where a snowy owl makes a dress of black and white feathers for Raven. Raven was so excited by the beautiful dress that he wouldn't stand still for the fitting. The owl after many attempts to calm Raven became so frustrated that she threw some oil on the bird, dying Raven black all over. Raven has remained black until this day.

In one tale from the Northwest the peacock and Raven are friends. They agree to paint each other's feathers. The peacock looks at his reflection in a pool and is thrilled by Raven's artistic skills. Deciding he does not want competition from Raven, he paints the white bird black. And so all ravens remain black to this day, although the sheen of white can be seen shining through the black feathers in the right light.

The Sioux tell the story of how a white raven would warn the buffalo of approaching hunters, causing the buffalo to stampede and leaving the Sioux hungry. Eventually, an angry shaman threw the bird into the fire, turning the raven black as it remains to this day. In this story the raven is far from a sacred otherworldly being.

The following legend from the Northwest has a moral point imbedded in it.

Great Spirit Eagle is painting birds along the banks of a river. He has just finished painting Raven's feathers and is leaving. Raven doesn't like the way he looks so he begs a beautiful Eagle who is nearby to paint his feathers anew from the paints the Great Spirit has left in the river. "I want to look beautiful like you," Raven begs, and Eagle finally agrees. Eagle paints Raven white and is pleased with his artistic handiwork, but Raven upon seeing his reflection in the river is furious. "I am uglier than before," he caws. Raven and Eagle fight eventually spilling all the Great Spirit's paints over Raven. Raven jumps into the river and flaps his wings as fast as he can but the blackness of the wet paints will not fade from his feathers. Seconds later the Great Spirit returned. Raven tells the Great Spirit of his fight with Eagle and begs him to restore his original painting of the feathers. The Great Spirit refuses and says, "Because of your sin of envy you shall learn to value what you have. From this day forward you will remain with black beak, black feet, black breast, and black eyes."

I get another cup of coffee and return to the deck, laughing to myself about all the different stories about Raven turning black. I am reminded of a most complex myth on how Raven becomes black. The myth reveals the mysticism and majesty of Raven Creator, struggles with his dark nature, and foreshadows his trickster characteristics.

In this story it is out of the fog mythical Raven arises, coming from nowhere and not bound by time, space, or physical limitations. It is my favorite creation myth.

A little background before the sharing of the story:

In Native American mythology, physical Raven remains spiritual but also bound by the needs and desires of earthly life. He lives between the physical and the spiritual, a foot planted in both realities. In the following myth, all flows from Raven's creation. This is one of the few myths that relates Raven turning black to the story of creation.

The myth is called "Why Raven is Black and the World Imperfect." As with all folktales, legends, and myths, changes in the story take place over time showing the thinking of a new storyteller relating the myth to the current situation. It is like the marginal writings attached to the Torah where notes from the translator priests are placed next to the Torah. Such notes respond to the contemporary problems and add new insight to the Torah. Over time the notes, called *midrash*, gain as much authority as the Torah itself. Midrash is hermeneutic.

As with midrash, changes in Native American stories are inevitable, expected, and reveal the living dynamic of mythology and legend as it is applied hermeneutically to the current situation. Different tribes often tell the same story line with a variety of specifics. As all stories, this one has experiences changes and new interpretations over time.

The mythical tale:

In early time before man was upon the earth, Raven was, shining white as pure snow, radiant, glistening in the sunlight and glowing with the moon. The soul of Raven was pure, filled with love, light, and beauty.

But Raven was not alone. His twin brother was physically beautiful, and yet, his feathers like his soul were dark as the deepest night, a night without moon or stars. A night full of fear, uncertainty, and absent of trust and compassion. Love was foreign to the black raven.

White Raven relished in creating beauty and filling all life with happiness. When he laughed, all his creation laughed with him—the sun shone brighter, animals frolicked, and trees whistled as the warm wind blew through them. Majestic mountains affirmed to all living beings—life is good.

Not all on earth was joyful. White Raven's dark brother created as well, but his creations were ugly and abhorrent. The Dark One created monsters, leeches, and poisonous snakes. His creations reflected his own mean spirit. He took pleasure in destroying the creations of White Raven. His dark angry heart extended into every aspect of his being and to every outward expression.

One day the dark twin frightened White Raven as he was completing one of his most graceful and beautiful creations, the deer. To this day the deer is skittish and moves quickly away when fear is sensed.

White Raven was so busy concentrating on his own creations that he gave very little attention to what Black Raven was doing. He was sure Black Raven's actions towards him were the result of bad moods, poor timing, or, perhaps, a lack of sleep. But the evil of the Dark One was more than a temporary state or a misunderstanding; evil was his essence.

One afternoon when White Raven was putting the finishing touches on a perfectly designed fish, Black Raven jumped out from a hiding place and stomped on the yet to be painted fish. The Dark One crushed the fish, resulting in a flat, unappealing shape that became the first flounder.

On another day the Black Twin spotted White Raven in deep concentration, carefully painting the delicate colors on Puffin. Dark Raven quietly snuck up to the paint box, smeared the colors into the ground and destroyed the cedar box in which White Raven kept his valued paints.

"What is going on?" shouted White Raven, finally reaching the end of his tolerance. "Why do you want to hurt and destroy? If you do it again, I will surely kill you."

"Ha," responded the Dark One. "There is only one thing that can kill me. You know what it is because it is the same thing that can kill you, an axe."

"That's not true," said the White Raven. "Maybe an axe can kill you, but the only thing that can kill me is a whip." This, of course, was a lie. A lie motivated by a growing suspicion that the Dark One was planning to kill him. The White Raven tricked his brother into believing a whip was the only weapon that could bring death to him.

That very night, as moonlight reflected with a warm glow on the sleeping White Raven, the Dark One approached in silence. And then, in an instant, the movement of calm air in the relaxed and quiet darkness was shattered by the crack of a whip.

White Raven shouted in pain as the whip hit his side, slicing three feathers apart. He looked up in pain and anger to see his brother standing above him. "Is there no limit to your evil?" cried White Raven. Quickly moving, he grabbed a hidden axe he had placed under his bed earlier that evening fearing his brother might try to kill him. Before the Dark One could respond, White Raven planted the axe deep into his brother's skull. Blood flew from the black bird, covering much of the room as well as White Raven in gore. Within an instant, the great bird was white no more, but shining black from his brother's blood.

White Raven watched his dark brother take his last breath and his heart was overcome with remorse. White Raven was a lover of life. "I have lived only to create life, beauty, and happiness; and now, I have killed my own brother. What have I become?" He looked down at his mountain making hands in disgust and shame. He who had only created life and beauty had now destroyed his own brother. White Raven knew he would never be the same again.

Looking at his blood-stained black feathers, he felt darkness grip his heart and soul. Try as he might to remove the stain from his feathers, he could not. The soul of his lost twin had entered the White Raven in places where good and light once reigned alone. Overwhelmed with deep sadness and grief, he swore he would never again create. Then he withdrew from the world.

Raven lost himself in the dense forest of the Northwest. There he wandered for forty days and nights, examining what had become of him. "Who am I? How can I create now that I have destroyed?" bemoaned the remorseful killer. "And what of my quest to make the most perfect creature filled with compassion, wisdom and love, living in awe of beauty and gratitude for life. I was going to call it a human being," he had thought. "I cannot create perfection as I myself am now filled with contradiction. I feel darkness, coldness in my heart; my twin has become one with me. I still love all living things, and yet I have killed my own brother. No longer am I just filled with love." And he continued to wander lost in his thoughts.

Raven's appearance had changed forever. His feathers were permanently dyed a shining black with his brother's blood even though the original white brilliance would show through in his feathers from time to time if the light was just right.

Raven knew his appearance as well as his nature would never be as they once were. Where there had been only compassion, love and joy, now they were accompanied by cunning, mischief, and greediness. Before the goodness reigned supreme; now there were moments when cunning, destruction, greed, and even trickery would prevail over good. His body, once bright with white feathers, brilliant as the sun, was now clothed in feathers of deepest black, shining, shimmering mirrors of jet and the dazzling sheen of diamonds, reflecting both the daylight and moonlight. Raven lives the contradictory realities of good and evil, life and death, beauty and ugliness, finitude and eternity.

Raven dwelt in the silence and stillness of the encompassing woods. He listened to his breath drawn from outside himself and becoming part of him when he inhaled.

As time passed in the forest, the silence and stillness brought insight. Raven gained a balance between the contradictory parts of his heart and soul. He realized that conflicting emotions, feelings, thoughts, and acts can reside in one being. Each living thing was capable of both hurting and helping. Slowly the desire to finish making the world and creating Human Beings returned, although they would now be imperfect. This is a good thing, he came to realize. The contradiction within him became a paradox to be balanced. The effort of living would be more challenging with these paradoxes. He now understood if everything was perfect it would be boring, because of no contrast. There would be no free will if everything was perfect and could be nothing but perfect. Such perfection would be a curse.

When Raven walked out of the dense forest, the first thing he did was try to make human beings. As with his own newly acquired nature, Raven had a hard time with consistency in his creations. Some people were too tall, others too short. Sometimes he made them physically beautiful, but they would have terrible tempers. Other times they would come out clever but use it for greedy purposes. In all cases they had contradictory characteristics, just like their Creator. They had an eternal quality but were bound by the finite. Even with his new perspective found in the wilderness, not being able to create a perfect human being frustrated Raven.

In the midst of his frustration he had a revelation. "You know," he reminded himself, "Maybe human beings aren't supposed to be perfect. Maybe they are by nature a combination of good and evil, wise and silly, beautiful and ugly, trustworthy and tricky. I need to pause, take a deep breath, and remember what I learned in the deep forest. Maybe I shouldn't be so critical of my work but just accept people the way they are. Since my brother and I now share one soul full of contradictions, maybe this is the nature of things. And maybe, just maybe, human beings are coming out better and more interesting than the perfect human being I so desired to create but that has eluded me. I can now see the contradictions becoming paradoxes when they are blended together in my creations."

So Raven finally and forever gave up on the idea of creating perfection. Everything he created, people and creatures of all kinds, had a dual nature; they were both good and bad. For example, the beaver was hardworking but chewed down trees where birds once lived and damned up water people needed to grow food. The skunk was beautiful but, at times, he really stank. And even Raven Creator's direct descendants, ravens, while clever, smart, and beautiful were also destroyers, tricksters, and gluttons. "It is better this way," thought Raven. "Life is more interesting, more challenging, and filled with adventures and laughter that would not be there if all I created was perfect."

I take a swig of my now cold coffee as my thoughts leave the myth I have come to love. I wonder if the great Swiss psychiatrist and psychoanalyst Carl Jung was familiar with this particular story of the black and white Raven brothers? If he wasn't, I believe he would have liked it. Carl Jung viewed the raven as symbolic of the dark side of the psyche. He acknowledged, as does much raven mythology, that we have two sides to us and we were created this way. We have both the dark and light within that can lead to wisdom as well as trickery and the potential of destruction.

My wife, Joy, breaks my thought trance and calls me into dinner. She has been supportive and kind to me this strange day spent totally on the deck. We share a fresh chicken salad as the bright sun fades and is replaced by the soft light of the moon shimmering on the lake.

After dinner I pour myself a shot of Jameson's Black Barrel, turn on the electric fireplace, plop myself down into the familiar feel of my long serving rocker, and begin to sip the 'nectar of the gods.' What an adventure today has been for me even though I never left our place and rarely moved from the deck. I smile and let my mind relax and wander....

It was Winter, 1962, as I settled into my sophomore year at a small Christian college in Eugene, Oregon. My life was good. I was Sophomore Class President, doing okay, not great with grades, and held a weekend job as a youth minister at a church in Portland, an hour and a half north of Eugene. I had purchased my first car several months earlier, a salmon colored 1955 Oldsmobile 88, that allowed me to take the job in Portland while providing an independence that made me feel like I was an adult.

Generally, four fellow students would join me on the Friday ride from our college to their homes in Portland and return with me on Sunday night. This weekend was different. All four rode with me to Portland but decided to stay an extra day and return with a parent on Monday evening.

I left Portland alone on Sunday night for the quiet, pleasant drive back to Eugene. It was finals week at the college and the University of Oregon where I also took classes. My mind was pre-occupied with the challenge the next week presented to me academically.

It was 11:30 p.m., that fateful night, when my life changed forever. A man living in Portland had learned Sunday morning that his father had died. He put his life and belongings in order, got in his brand new Chevrolet

Impala, and headed for Phoenix, Arizona, for his father's funeral. He planned to drive all night. As he drove away from his home, I was leaving Portland for my routine drive back to Eugene.

A little before midnight, the life of this man I never knew collided with mine. He was lost in thought of his father, driving on the almost empty freeway at 120 miles per hour, when he plowed into my car forcing it into a car in front of mine. The trunk of my car was crushed against my dashboard. Miraculously, no one was seriously hurt, except me. I was covered up for dead at the side of the road.

The ambulance took me to the Lebanon, Oregon, hospital that became my home for the next two weeks as I recuperated from severe head wounds.

In the midst of my medical and mental confusion, each morning from my new multi-movement bed I would look out my second story window and wait for the ravens to arrive. Like clockwork with the coming of the sun they would appear cawing in playful delight. They danced among tree branches, stopped to rest, played some more, then cawed and flew off to their next adventure, only to return the next morning and perform the ritual anew.

I anxiously awaited the corvids return each day with the early morning light. I believed they helped me heal and knew they made me smile. My feeling of kinship with them was not returned as they remained indifferent and unaware of my very existence.

Fifty-six years later the memory of the hospital ravens remains vivid in my mind. It was my first personal encounter with Raven, but it would not be my last. Raven was to become the central symbol of my life's paradoxes and transformations.

My serious head injuries healed physically, but I couldn't think straight. I tried taking finals after returning to school but failed them all. I was out of school for a year. I spent the next year living in the college dorm but not attending classes.

In my naïve manner, I settled with the insurance claim for $1,500, thinking that was a fortune. In my innocence I was tricked into taking far less than the expenses I incurred.

A few weeks after my accident, a straight "A" student, loaded with talent and charisma, was in a car wreck and killed. From that point on I never believed the words I had heard repeatedly since my wreck: "God has saved you for something important." If so, what about my dead friend? Was my personal God a great trickster and not to be trusted? The seeds of doubt in my conservative religious faith were beginning to grow.

I was vaguely aware at the time that my life had changed forever. The seed challenging my inherited worldview was planted. The social and religious fabric of my life had torn.

Over time I began to understand my imbedded childhood religious beliefs were challenged by the accident. Beliefs that defined me as an individual and provided a family and social basis for my life were suspect. I had lived in a wonderful world, where a loving personal God made things right and was always there. This was no longer self-evident to me. Life was no longer simply defined. God wasn't always there.

As White Raven turned black, I too examined the paradox of right and wrong, good and evil, material and spiritual, fair and unfair, trust and deception. I changed colors in the hospital bed, but did not acknowledge it.

Jameson gone, I hop into bed ready for a good night's sleep. There arrives in my mind what I call 'roof-brain chatter.' I can't get my mind to stop reflecting on the thoughts of the day. It will not relax and let me sleep. I keep wondering how does the ancient symbol of the mandorla that speaks to life's paradoxes, relate to Raven mythology and to my life.

CHAPTER TWO: RAVEN AS MANDORLA

The world breaks everyone and afterward many are strong in the broken places. But those that will not break it kills. It kills the very good and the very gentle and the very brave impartially. If you are none of these you can be sure it will kill you too but there will be no special hurry.

A Farewell to Arms by Ernest Hemingway

It is not that the light element alone does the healing; the place where light and dark begin to touch is where miracles arise. The middle place is a mandorla.

Owning Your Own Shadow by Robert A. Johnson

We are all familiar with Star Wars. The Jedi played by different rules and lived in two realities, the material and the spiritual. The once Jedi, Darth Vader, had a seed of the good in him. Luke Skywalker, Darth Vader's son, supplemented his goodness with a touch of the dark side. As father and son they shared one blood. Both breathed the same air. Darth Vader breathed in a frightening and destructive manner while Luke Skywalker breathed in a normal fashion. Both men contained the seed of their opposite.

It's 5:00 a.m. I wake, jump out of bed, and head for the coffee pot. Ten minutes later, cup in hand, I am back on the deck looking at my computer with my mind still focused on my last thought before sleep, the mandorla.

The stars silently cast a subtle light on my deck as they sparkle above in vivid contrast to the night sky. It will be a glorious dawn in an hour or so; I can feel it. The aroma of the lake and the smells of late Spring forest fill the air as I turn on my computer.

The computer kicks into gear and I begin to write:

On the cover of this book Raven is pictured with both black and white blended into his body. His body is shaped by two subtle circles overlapping and is, therefore, almond shaped. The White Raven present in the background of the painting is representative of the Spirit World while Black Raven represents the physical world. They do not supplement each other but are part of One. The Black Raven has an undercoating of white symbolic of the blending of the two worlds. The painting is both physically logical and magical, showing both the spiritual and the mundane. It is a mandorla.

Raven floats on the cusp of the spirit and material worlds with access to both. He exists before time and is a glutton who will lie and steal for a red berry. His eyes reflect the creative and destructive nature of his character while the red berry is symbolic of his never ending appetite. He places the sun in the material world through magical other worldly powers. He spreads his wings and is carried by the wind between the world of the finite and the world of myth.

The mandorla is easily mistaken for the Sanskrit word "mandala" which is a circle representing the wholeness or oneness of all things. Mandala represents the universe in Hindu and Buddhist symbolism. The less familiar word "mandorla" is our focus.

Mandorla is Italian and literally means "almond." The mandorla is created by two partially overlapping circles. When two contrasting bodies of belief partially overlap, the overlap creates a shape that looks like an almond, hence a mandorla. Each circle represents an opposing body of belief or opposites that are blended into one in the mandorla.

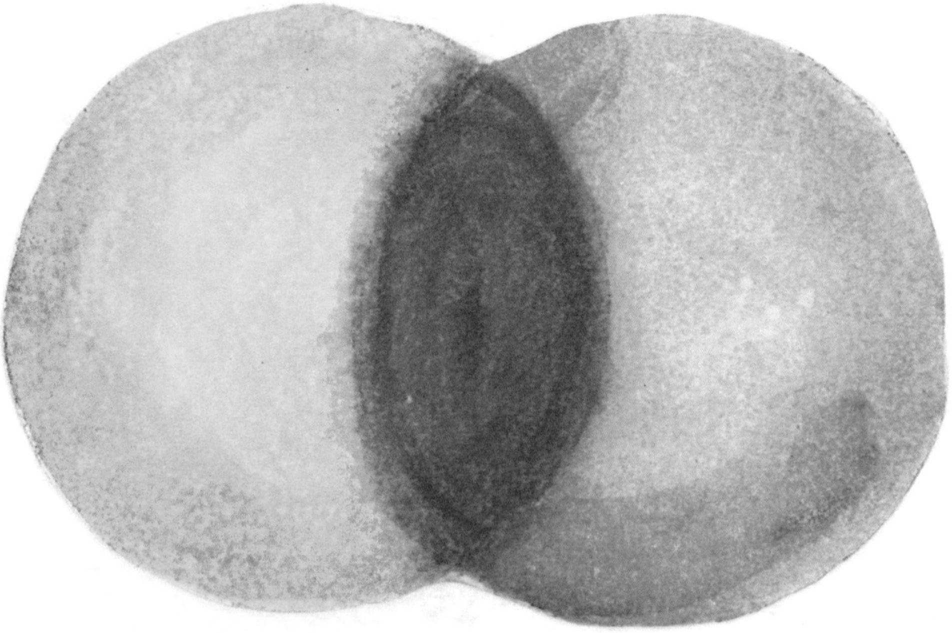

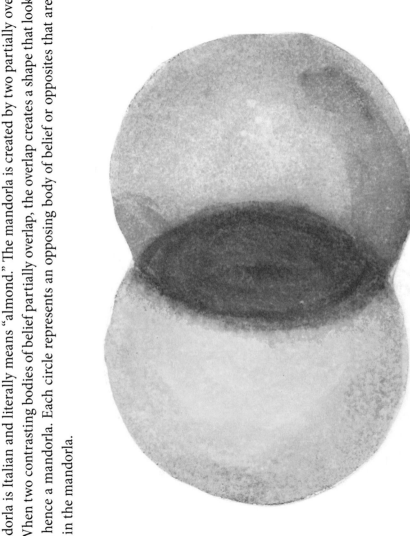

Mandorla, courtesy of the artist, Joy Cobbs

The mandorla is not dissimilar from the Chinese Yin and Yang. In both, different and seemingly contradictory realities overlap bringing to light paradoxes such as creation/destruction, life/death, good/evil, joy/suffering, and spiritual/physical. In each part of yin and yang and the mandorla the core element of its opposite is present. There is a paradox of simultaneous unity/duality in both yin and yang and the mandorla. When there is balance between the two opposites there is harmony, integrity, and insight into our own lives and the world.

The Native American Raven myth of the two brothers is reminiscent of the ancient symbols. The White Raven kills his brother and struggles with the contradictions that now reside within him. The Lakota Sioux author, Louis Two Ravens Irwin, in his autobiography, Two Ravens: The Life and Teachings of a Spiritual Warrior, recognizes that the greatest battles take place between the enemies within us. He speaks of ancient teachings showing the "way of ways" to find balance within oneself. After an angry and disruptive youth, Two Ravens found balance, the mandorla, through the Sun Dance ceremony and other ancient rituals. Darkness was his teacher, guiding him to live in the light with wisdom and perspective.

Stories of twins abound in the world's mythologies. Within these myths there is attraction, repulsion, resolution, individuation, sameness, opposites, and other contradictory concepts that are hard to wrap one's mind around. These are tensions everyone on the planet experiences.

Two Ravens understood darkness that cannot be rejected for the sake of light because everything contains its opposite. The mandorla is on the cusp of the spiritual and physical worlds, placing into dialogue two realities that seem irreconcilable. The mandorla takes us to the place where all opposites meet, engage, and inform each other.

The concept of the mandorla is also found in Hebrew Scripture. Isaiah 45:7 reads: "I am Yahweh, and there is no other. I form light and create darkness, I do peace and I create evil, I am Yahweh and I do all these things."

This same understanding of the mandorla is represented in ancient Greek mythology. Apollo often wore the title "Oulios." Originally the title meant 'deadly', 'cruel', or 'destructive.' Like the mythical brother Ravens, Apollo reveals that every god has a destructive side, and yet, he was associated with healing and medicine. Apollo was an intermediary between gods and men. The Greeks understood Apollo as the Northwest Indians understood Raven: the destroyer is the same who makes things whole, the destroyer who heals and the healer who destroys.

I believe the story of White Raven killing his brother can best be understood as White Raven killing the destructive part of himself only to find that it remains part of him, informing his life and giving him new insight and perspective.

The morning chill on the deck is fading away and with it the coming of a beautiful sunlit dawn. I think back to the year following my car accident. I was not physically able to attend classes; but, I continued to live on campus. Periodically, I would go into a small music practice room located in the library. The room had no windows and a lock on the door so I could be completely alone.

I possessed no musical ability, but I could use the space to pray (or beg) that I might have the secure belief that so many of my fellow students seemed to have. I would pray for understanding on why my classmate died and I lived. Nothing. No insight. No direction. I left such self-inflicted sessions more alone and confused than when I entered. After a half dozen visits I stopped going to the room.

I was angry and felt unattached to all I had been taught about God. Over time, I realized part of my religious tradition continued to inform my perspective on life, but it was no longer the only influence. I had to make room for my classmate's untimely death, contradictions in my life, and conflicting emotions within me. Now there were the ingredients for a mandorla. Now there was an opening for Raven.

Opportunity for insight and personal growth is enhanced when we face the contradictions within. When we deny, ignore, or bury part of who we are we "live in the shadows," and are not honest with ourselves.

HISTORY OF THE MANDORLA

In Christian art the mandorla is an aureole of light encompassing the entire figure of a holy person. It is often used around the figure of Christ. While the mandorla's origin is unknown, it first appears in the West in the fifth century in the Church of Sanrita Maria Maggiore in Rome where it surrounds some Old Testament figures. The mandorla symbolizes the good and evil in us and the paradox of the spiritual and physical realities present in even holy men.

The mandorla appears in the beginning of the Book of John: "In the beginning was the Word, and the Word was with God, and the Word was God. He was in the beginning with God; all things were made through him, and without him was not anything made that was made. In him was life, and the life was the light of men. The light shines in the darkness, and the darkness has not overcome it" (John 1:1-5). "The Word became flesh and dwelt among us…" (John 1:14). The light does not overcome darkness or vice versa. The two opposites reside together.

The mandorla removes condemnation of either the dark or the light. In the mandorla they are one and, through this oneness, inform the world in ways not possible if they remain separate. When the Word becomes flesh the spiritual and physical are understood as dwelling together, becoming one, informing and defining each other.

The words in the beginning of the book of John are not foreign to Native American understanding of the spiritual and the physical. White Raven, after becoming black, experienced this blending in his reflective time in the forest. He eventually removed any guilt for being not 'perfect' (whatever that is) and learned from the blending of opposites. He came to understand that his brother was really part of him and must be assimilated. Raven then is ready to be the mediator and messenger between the spiritual and physical worlds.

The Sun tells me it is now past 10:00 a.m. I do not want to leave the deck (except I do need another cup of Joe). Raven speaks inside my head: "I am enjoying listening to your thoughts today. Like my experience in the wilderness, I hope you are able to balance your paradoxes, your fears and tensions with hopes and comforts. Remember, all have a place inside of you. They are all part of one. I think you are slowly learning worldly goods should not overpower the intangibles in life, and yet, tangibles are required to sustain life. Balance will serve you well in this, the last stage of your life."

"Yes, Raven," I respond as I pour another cup, "I used to see my life as a continual choice between right and wrong, much like the white raven. It left me very judgmental of anyone who didn't think like I did. Living with contradiction and paradox was a curse, so I kept my conflicting thoughts in the shadows. Living in the shadows was a bigger curse. Now I see that the paradoxes in life make it both challenging and interesting. Life decisions are not cut and dried. I have learned, and am still learning, to be more tolerant of different thinking than my own and to face myself with honesty.

"Excited living comes in directly facing my own contradictions, experiencing life as challenging, and learning and growing from sharing with others. This is especially true when I am open to people with whom I disagree. I initially thought being open to new ideas showed no backbone, no courage of my convictions, but now I am starting to see myself as a student. I like to think of this as beginning to live within the almond."

Raven had listened respectfully to my thought response. Now he left my head with no further comment.

There is a wonderful and very familiar story of Raven hanging the Sun. The story has been told with many variations by many tribes. The basic message is hanging light in the darkness. Some of the trickster side of Raven also surfaces.

Before Raven hangs the sun there is only darkness, a world Raven finds impossible to live in. There is no opposite to the darkness. It is impossible to blend dark and light into one when only dark resides. Light must be found and balanced with dark to create a clear view of life and one's self.

The following is a version of the myth:

Long ago darkness covered the earth. Raven, Creator of the World, stumbled in the darkness and stubbed his toe. "That's enough of all this fumbling around in blackness. I must do something about it," Raven muttered in his pain.

Raven examined his bruised toe as well as he could in the darkness. It hurt and was cold. He fluffed his feathers and hunkered down, carefully placing warm, soft feathers over the injured digit. As he crouched on the hard ground, Raven thought to himself and remembered the beautiful daughter of an ugly and selfish old man. He had heard stories about this old man, about how he had a collection of boxes, each one nestled inside of the other. Inside the smallest of these boxes was the relief to the suffering of darkness. The box contained light, light hidden in the darkness or shadow of the smallest box.

Raven remembered that this beautiful girl had long and flowing hair, hair as glossy and lustrous as the Raven's wing, and lived in a cedar house beside a river. Raven wanted to learn more about the girl and was extremely curious about the rumors of her grandfather's boxes.

Raven pulled his injured foot up closer to his body and balanced on one leg. After dozing and warming his foot, he stretched his wings and flew up into the sky, and the wind guided him to the cedar house.

As Raven approached the cedar house, he heard the thin voice of the old man singing about his beloved boxes. The man sang of cedar boxes nestled within cedar boxes, and the wonderful treasure secreted within the smallest box. Hearing the singing, Raven knew that he had found the right place. An accomplished thief, Raven thought that it would be easy to steal the box of light and destroy the old man's selfish hoarding in the process. The challenge would be getting access to the house.

Raven's mind turned and turned as he perched high in the branches of a hemlock tree outside the cedar house. As Raven roosted, plotting, the old man's daughter came out of the house carrying a basket for water. Raven scrutinized her form, and his sharp ears registered her footsteps. As she walked to the stream, Raven flapped his wings and flew through the trees. The darkness hid him from the girl.

Raven the Shape-shifter/Trickster had devised a scheme to get into the cedar house. He flew upstream from the innocent maiden, changed himself into a hemlock needle, and floated down into the gently moving waters. As the girl dipped her basket into the cool, running water, Raven was caught. The girl took a strong, deep drink, and Raven, the hemlock needle, slid down her throat and into her belly. Raven then found a soft place deep in the girl's womb, bundled himself in the warmth, and magically transformed into a fetus.

All of this transformation made Raven sleepy, and he curled up for a long nap. He slept for several months in the warm bundle womb as his fetus-form grew and developed into a healthy boy-child. He was normal in all ways, except that he had a beak-like protuberance covered with skin for his nose. Finally, he came forth from the girl in the same way as human children. Naturally, the girl loved the little Raven-baby, although in the darkness she could not see him well. The old man, Raven-baby's grandfather, loved his daughter, and naturally, doted on his grandson, too.

It was indeed greedy and selfish of the old man to hoard the world's light. On the other hand, the old man was very kind to Raven-baby who he truly loved. The old man sang songs to him and cuddled him and made all kinds of toys for him.

Of course, Raven was mindful of his mission, the freeing of the light and, with his bright and shiny raven-eyes, was constantly peering around the cedar house, looking for those boxes within boxes. A huge carved cedar box stood in one corner of the house. After much study, Raven was convinced that this must be the box containing all the other boxes, and the light.

Raven-boy toddled over to the box. Despite his human form, he still had a slight waddle when he walked, the same waddle ravens have when they walk on the ground in the deep woods. Raven looked around to be sure that he was alone—the girl and her father had walked down to the stream together. But just as Raven lifted the lid of the big box, the old man walked in and scolded Raven-boy for touching his most prized possession. He told him never to touch that box again, thus confirming Raven's suspicion that he had indeed found the light box.

From that day on, Raven-boy constantly cajoled his grandfather to give him the big, carved cedar box. When the old man said no, Raven-boy howled and cried and begged some more. Finally, the old man, out of love for the child, relented, and taking other, smaller boxes from inside, gave him the outer box. Raven-boy continued to cajole and one by one, he accumulated the other boxes.

In time, Raven had been given all of the boxes except the smallest one containing the light. A glow emanated from the box, and Raven-boy demanded it, too, as a gift from his grandfather.

"Absolutely not," Grandfather said. Raven-boy started crying. He howled and yowled.

"Give it to me, give it to me. I want the box. I want to see inside," he squawked.

Finally, the old man relented. He opened the box and tossed it to Raven-boy. In an instant, Raven-boy transformed into his old self, swooped down upon the light, took it in his beak, and flew up on the wind through the smoke hole in the ceiling of the cedar house and out into the open sky.

Raven flew higher and higher. Eventually he reached a place where he broke off a large piece of the light and placed it in the dark sky. Raven called it "Sun." The light shone in the darkness, and the darkness did not overcome it.

Looking back over his shoulder, he saw the girl, his virgin mother, in sunlight for the first time. She was indeed very beautiful. As Raven flew carrying the light in his beak, he saw the world that he had created. He saw the stark and rugged mountains, trees, boulders and rivers, and the villages of men, with their carved cedar poles chronicling the history of the clans. Raven enjoyed the beauty of his creation even as he reflected on destroying the contentment of the old man and his daughter.

Suddenly, Raven felt a shadow and saw the talons of a big eagle close to him. Startled, Raven opened his beak and dropped the remainder of the light. It hit the earth and broke into two pieces. The largest piece bounced up into the air and became the moon. Raven retrieved the other piece of light, and carrying it in his beak, flew beyond the boundaries of earth and sky and pushed the light out, far away from earth where it broke into small pieces and became stars.

Raven returned to the sun and moon and put them in exactly their proper places where the sun warmed, gave light, and sustained all life even to this day. And the moon at night, along with the stars, provided some light and revealed the beauty of the universe.

In this old story the sun and other heavenly bodies do not remove the darkness, they supplement it. Without darkness there would be no context for light. Everything contains its opposite. Even Raven betrays the grandfather and his virgin mother to secure the light needed by the world.

In the earlier myth White Raven was not complete until he realized and accepted that part of him was Dark Raven. Such opposite binding is the essence of the story and of reality. As the late Robert A. Johnson wrote, "If the two extremes can be woven together to make a masterpiece, perhaps I can bring the ragged, disjointed elements of my own life together."[3] The story of Raven securing and placing light in darkness makes the same point.

Healing comes forth from the overlap of light and dark. Raven places the sun in the darkness in part to see more clearly and not hurt himself again. It is not that the light element alone heals; the place where light and dark meld together is where miracles arise.

In the mandorla we place paradoxical aspects of ourselves into conversation, and from this gain insight into our lives and the world. The mandorla has no place for remorse. It requires conscious work of us. It is not self-indulgence or defensiveness.

The theologian Robert Johnson once again informs our understanding: "Guilt is also a cheap substitute for paradox. The energy consumed by guilt would be far better invested in the courageous act of looking at the two sets of truths that have collided in our personality. Guilt is also arrogant because it means we have taken sides in an issue and are sure we are right. While this one-sidedness may be part of the cultural process, it is severely detrimental to the religious life. To lose the power of confrontation is to lose one's chance at unity—and to miss the healing power of the mandorla." [4]

We can view our lives as a mandorla. Our human condition divides us again and again into opposite conflicting sides in our lives. When opposites inside us are confronted honestly, reconciliation and new understandings can arise. It is a daily challenge to live in the mandorla. The mandorla is not the place of neutrality or compromise; it is the place of the peacock's tail and rainbows, blending opposites into new beauty.

Joy brings me a ham and cheese sandwich, some grapes, and a glass of water. "You've had enough coffee for one day," she says with a smile. "And it is 2:30 p.m., way past time for you to eat something. You must really be

---

[3] Owning Your Own Shadow by Robert Johnson. HarperCollins Publisher, Sydney, Austrailia. 2013, p. 110.)

[4] Owning Your Own Shadow, by Robert Johnson, HarperCollins Publisher, Sydney Australia, 2013. P. 118)

lost in thought to wait this long to eat. You are always hungry." I smile and think: Ah gluttony, always hungry, ready to steal or lie for food. This is a fundamental characteristic of immortal Raven.

Raven is contradiction. Of such is folklore. Of such is mandorla. If one wishes a clear systematic, never contradictory deity or spiritual messenger, it is not found in Raven. Raven presents the great Creator, the angry and nonchalant Destroyer, and the gluttonous and self-centered Trickster caring only for himself.

In folklore the most engaging character in storytelling is the Trickster. With all the heroes, monsters, and lovers, it is the Trickster who draws the interest of most readers.

CHAPTER THREE: THE TRICKSTER BIRD

Tricksters are "on the road." They are the lords of in-between....Trickster is the mythic embodiment of ambiguity and ambivalence, doubleness and duplicity, contradiction and paradox.[5]

The Ashanti people of Ghana had Anansi. The Norse had Loki. They're all mythological figures that taught humanity how quick thinking could enliven and enrich the species. Also high on the honor roll: Hermes (ancient Greece), Reynard (France), Bugs Bunny (Looney Tunes). The twenty-first century U.S.A. has Mr. William Murray, our modern-day trickster god.[6]

A few days ago I was walking on the lakeshore when I spotted an osprey flying over the lake. The osprey examined the lake and then dived like a falling rock, broke the surface of the water, remained submerged for thirty seconds, and resurfaced with a large trout in his beak. A family of ravens appear from nowhere, cawing and chasing the osprey. The osprey attempted to evade the ravens and still hold onto the trout. The ravens circled and acted as if they would attack the osprey. Their actions had a playful quality although the osprey did not see it that way.

The ravens drove the osprey away from the lake and over the land where it eventually dropped the fish and flew away. The last I saw the ravens they were swooping down to the landlocked trout where I assumed they feasted in style and personal satisfaction with their successful escapade.

TRICKSTER IN FOLKLORE

In folklore and especially legends, Trickster is a character in a story having intellect or knowledge others don't have, and uses it to play tricks or disobey normal rules and conventional behavior. The Trickster can be a supernatural or the mischievous being who can change shapes to gain what he wants. He will cause chaos

[5] Trickster Makes the World by Lewis Hyde, Straus and Giroux Publishing, New York. p. 7

[6] The Tao of Bill Murray by Gavin Edwards and R. Sikoryak, Random House, Canada. 2016. p. 5.

while, at the same time, inspiring some kind of change to take place. He can outwit anyone, but often is his own worst enemy. The Trickster mocks authority and acts out of impulse.

In legends told throughout time and around the world of courageous heroes, monsters that challenge them, and innocents to be saved, it is the trickster that steals the show. The trickster is universal and ancient. The Greek God Hermes is called *mechaniota* which means "trickster." The Western African trickster, *Legha*, means, "I have tricked you." And the Winnebago Indian figure *Wakdjunkago* is known as "the tricky one."

The trickster wants to soothe his appetite, whether it is for someone else's food, wife, or the thrill of getting something for nothing. He will do anything to fulfill his selfish needs, including changing shape and gender. The trickster never apologizes or feels guilty, even when he is "caught in the act." He is neither moral nor immoral, he is in-between. The trickster is amoral.

In European legends and fairy tales, Trickster is not a central character. Rather, he is relegated to a minor role and generally appears as a male human. In contrast, Native American stories and legends often make Trickster the main character and, while almost always a nonhuman male, he is generally a talking animal who, when it suits his purpose, will assume human form. At other times Trickster, as a resident in the mythical world, will take on the shape of things like a tree leaf or twig to get where he wants to be and get what he desires.

Sometimes the trickster succeeds in outwitting others in ingenious ways, and sometimes he comes off as the fool. Often both happen in the same story. Such stories have delighted people for centuries. In our own time, the contemporary cartoon, "The Roadrunner," appeals to all of us. Wylie Coyote tries time after time to "trick" the roadrunner, alas, never to succeed.

Trickster forces society and individuals to continually question the status quo. So often Trickster ends up the fool, but in the process he challenges us to look anew at what is important to us. We stand in appreciation of Trickster's insights while laughing at his buffoonery. As a fool, Trickster reminds us of the importance of humor and playfulness and helps us see life from atypical perspectives.

It can be difficult to see Raven as Trickster after learning about all the great things he has done. And yet, as we have already discussed, Raven can be very mischievous and deceptive. This is true in legend as well as in his earthly life.

In earthly life ravens will hide food or even play dead to get what they want. They can be playful, using snow covered roads as slides and playing keep-away with other animals like wolves, otters, and dogs. Ravens will make toys using sticks, rocks and even stolen golf balls. They, without conscience, will deceive other animals and steal their food.

The Trickster Raven legends generally start out with Trickster's appetite, often for food, being recognized. The Raven plots to fill his appetite anyway possible. Raven then moves into action using creative deceit. And the stories end with the unmasking of Raven's deceit. There is a creative deception at its best, the wearing of a mask by pretending to be what he is not, then being caught and found to be a fool.

TRICKSTER AS RULE BREAKER

The trickster breaks rules and taboos. He is a rebel against established authority, and completely focused on fulfilling his own appetite. At the same time he offers fun, laughter, and even insight to those around him. He is what most of us at various times secretly wish we could be.

Trickster is creator and destroyer, giver and taker, he who cons and dupes others or who is conned or duped himself. He possesses no values yet it is through his actions values come into being.

As far back as time goes, tricksters have uncovered and disrupted the very things culture is based on. The Trickster understands the culture's social life and expression, which he challenges. He acts in the area where good and evil are confused, and he does so without choosing sides.

The Trickster has no one place he calls home. He does his tricking "on the road." The road the trickster travels is not just the road of earthly facts but the spirit road as well. He will steal not only from people but from the gods. He draws from the mythical world to do his trickery on earth. He is a boundary crosser.

With every group there is an "edge" that determines if people are in or out. The Raven Trickster lives on that edge. Every group determines right or wrong, clean or dirty, acceptable or unacceptable. Trickster will cross that line and confuse the definition of what is in and what is out. When moral behavior will keep someone from acting, tricksters suggest an amoral act that will get life going again. He doesn't play by the rules.

GREEDY TRICKSTER

For the Northwest Native Americans, Trickster Raven is both mischievous child and hero. He shifts his identity from story to story, and sometimes within the same story, from the clown to the creator of the world. Both are part of his essence.

The Raven Trickster is always hungry, ready to steal food and continuously lazy. Hence, he is always trying to quench some appetite for nothing and con others into doing all the work to obtain his goals. Raven can be childlike and manipulative to gain what he wants. He will do most anything to quench his appetite. He has perfected his ability to trick others through deceit and misdirection. He is a crafty creature who regularly disrupts the order of things, sometimes humiliating himself in the process.

PLAYFUL TRICKSTER

In our all too structured world, the Raven trickster represents chaos and freedom. He readily acknowledges his unfulfilled appetite. He is a being without philosophical purpose, never raising questions concerning the meaning of life.

And yet, the trickster informs all our lives, makes us laugh, helps us understand who we are, and clarifies the mores we live by.

Raven Trickster has for centuries provided fun and delight to young and old alike. We discover in the Trickster laughter, tears, fun, sadness, the power of all kinds of appetites, and a mirror on our culture and ourselves. All of this is hidden away in legends and folktales.

He is a model for independent behavior, a fun personality, and from time to time the savior of his people. The Raven's playful side reveals the incongruities and unpredictability of life in the tribal community and, indeed, in all our lives. While amoral himself, there is almost always a moral to be had in a trickster story.

Lest we idealize the life of a thief and liar, it must be mentioned that they are not tricksters at all. The actions of ordinary thieves and liars are not subtle and do not operate on a high plain. Raven is not your everyday run-of-the-mill thief. His goal is not to get rich but to disturb the status quo and fill his belly at the same time. His actions are close to what Picasso said of art, "Art is a lie that tells the truth." As the Trickster, Picasso was out to disrupt the world, challenge existing standards, and view life in a new form. The Trickster Raven's acts are deceptive, socially unacceptable, and like Picasso's art, truth-telling.

It is now afternoon with slight hint of dusk as I sit in my familiar chair on the deck to write some more about the loveable Raven as Trickster and how so many stories revolve around him stealing food. Speaking of stealing food, I am aware I am hungry again; I leave the deck and return with chips and onion dip. As I indulge in my snack this late sunny afternoon with not a cloud in sight, I watch children playing on the lake beach directly below me.

A few hundred years ago there were other children on another beach on the Lower Coast Salish of Vancouver Island. Stories were told on that coastal beach with children gathered around a grandparent eager to share a time honored tradition of storytelling, to continue passing the folklore from generation to generation.

"Grandfather, grandfather! Tell us a story," the children shout.

"What would you like to hear?" asks the elder with a smile.

"The one about the dogs," laugh the children as they announce their choice in unison.

Grandfather smiles and tells the story the children had heard a hundred times.

"There were a bunch of dogs trying to pick a king. Someone says, "Let's pick the dog who barks the loudest." The other dogs respond in unison, "No, it would be too loud, self-centered, and make the neighbor's mad."

"Well, how about we pick the biggest dog?" says another.

"No," says the crowd, "that is discrimination and we don't want that."

Then a little dog in the back of the group offers, "How about the dog that has the best smelling butt?"

"Great idea!" someone says and everyone agrees.

So all the dogs began to sniff each other's butts. As you can see when you happen upon two or more dogs, they still haven't found a king and are still sniffing butts."

The children howl with glee.

"Tell us another one, Grandfather. Please," the children shout as Raven caws in the distant background.

"You hear that?" asked the grandfather.

"No, what?" say the children.

The Raven caws again, only this time the sound is closer.

"That," says grandfather.

"Do you mean the raven making that sound?" the children ask.

Grandfather, wanting to tell a trickster story, says, "Yes. Raven. Let me tell you of the raven and his appetite for red berries."

One day in the early fall, when the salmon were running and the skies were bright and clear, allowing the sun to warm the earth, Raven and his little sisters, the crows, decided to go out and pick berries.

The rolling hills of southern Vancouver Island were thick with red berry bushes, and the beautiful berries were ripening under the sun's warm benediction. Raven told his sisters, the crows, that he knew just the place to find the ripest, most succulent berries in the hills behind a beach, a short canoe trip away from their home village.

So the little crows, happy at the prospect of a berry feast, eagerly gathered their food baskets and together with Raven, hopped from the beach into the big canoe.

Raven started out paddling the short distance to the red berry coves, but after a few minutes, announced that he was exhausted, too tired to paddle further. "After all," Raven told his sisters, "it is such a warm and sunny day. I am so sleepy. You take over and let me doze here in the canoe and I'll help you gather the berries from the hills when we get there."

So the crows took over the work of paddling while Raven sprawled out in the back of the cedar canoe and snoozed.

Raven awoke with a start when the canoe landed on the beach. "What, we're here already?" Raven mumbled. "I am so tired. Well, the bushes are right over there, you can't miss them; they are everywhere." Lazy Raven pointed towards the end of the beach where the forested hills began. Bushes, loaded with sweet, plump, juicy red berries lined the beach and extended through the forest thickets and up the hillsides as far as the eye could see.

"I would like to help you unload these big baskets," Raven gallantly said to his sisters. "But I am still so sleepy; let me rest here in the canoe for a while and soon I will come up and help you gather."

The industrious crows strapped their burden-baskets across their foreheads and headed up the beach and into the woods. Raven promptly went to sleep, awakening only when the sisters brought basket loads of the delicious red berries to the boat, where they dumped them and immediately returned to the berry-brambles to collect more. As each basket was emptied, Raven nibbled on the berries, eating one after another. Soon ravenous, gluttonous Raven gobbled each and every basket full of berries that his sisters brought to the canoe.

As the shadows lengthened, Raven realized that he had eaten the crows' entire day's work. He knew that his sisters would be upset and angry when they returned and discovered his obnoxious behavior. Raven knew he was going to have to make up a story to explain the disappearance of the berries.

In those days, enemy raiders were everywhere, and they would overtake the unwary, looting and killing. Raven knew that he would have to make up a truly horrific tale, one that invoked his sisters' fear of raiders, in order to cover his greedy tracks.

Plucking a few small tail feathers, he threw them into the surf and muttered an enchantment to make the feathers look like enemy war canoes.

Raven's chest was crimson from the juice of the berries he had gobbled, so he ruffled up his feathers and plucked out a few from his breast, making himself look disheveled and damaged. He scattered the few remaining berries and the cedar baskets and ran around making dozens of tracks to give the appearance of a struggle. Then he collapsed on the sandy beach beside the canoe and began to wail.

When the happy cawing crow sisters heard his moaning, they came running to him before they had a chance to fill their baskets with berries.

"Ow, ow, ow, ooooo…" Raven moaned. "What, am I still in this world? Oh, my sisters, I am so glad that you are safe." The crows crowded around Raven, concerned and worried.

"What happened? What happened?" they cried out in a chorus.

"Enemy raiders, it was terrible. I tried to fight them off, as you can see from the blood on my chest, but there were just too many of them. They took all of our berries and paddled away," Raven lied. "If you look out into the sea, you can see their war canoes."

Raven pointed toward the enchanted feathers, and the crows, out of love and concern, believed their brother. They thought that they saw enemy canoes. "Oh, our poor brother, we will bind your wounds and take you home," the worried crows cried.

Covering his face with his hands, as if in pain, Raven smiled a secret smile the crows could not see. His deception had worked. And indeed, his stomach was starting to hurt as a result of stuffing so many berries into it.

The crows loaded the canoes with their empty baskets; they were saddened by the loss of a full day's labor but happy their brother was safe and alive. They had turned to lift injured Raven into the canoe when a little snail called to them.

"Yoo-hoo, Crows, listen to me," little Snail called out to the homeward-bound group. "I have something to share with you, some news to tell you.

Snail crawled up to the canoe, and pointed directly at Raven. "Shame, shame on you, naughty Raven, for deceiving your sisters," the indignant Snail said. "I saw it all, I tell you, and there was no enemy raid. Your lazy brother gobbled up all of your berries, and then told you a lie to hide his greediness."

The crows' concern turned to anger when they learned they had been deceived. "How could you do this to us, Raven?" they asked. "Is it really true, what he tells us?"

"I saw what you did, and I'm telling," little Snail told Raven accusingly.

"Ummmmm....Well....look...you can see the canoes for yourself; little Snail is lying, not me," Raven said weakly. He pointed toward the canoes in the sea, but the enchantment had worn off, and the crows saw no canoes, only tail feather pieces, seeing them for what they really were. Upon close examination of Raven, they realized that he was covered with berry juice, not blood. The crows mobbed Raven and boxed his ears, and for his punishment, made him row all the way back to the village and explain to everyone why there would be no berries for supper.

"The raven was really tricky, but he got caught," says a young boy.

"How true," replies grandfather, "He gets caught a lot of the time, but not always. He can really be tricky."

"It is getting late so let me tell you another quick story about the tricky raven before you go to sleep."

The children draw closer. Grandfather tells a story that has its origin with the Tlingit tribe from Alaska and has been adapted by many other Northwest tribes.

"Raven happened by where many people were encamped, fishing on a lakeshore. Raven came to them and asked what they used for bait. They said, "Fat."

The ever hungry Raven asked, "Let me see you put enough fat on your hooks for bait." Raven noticed carefully how they baited and handled their hooks. The next time the fishermen went out to fish, Raven walked off behind the point where he could go underwater unseen by the fishermen. He then went after the bait. You see Raven was no ordinary bird. He could change into whatever shape he wished and could not only fly and walk, but could swim underwater as fast as any fish.

So Raven dived into the water where the fishermen were fishing. Raven would take the bait, making the fishermen think they had a bite. The fishermen would feel a tug on their fishing lines and pull up their poles, but there was no fish and no bait on the hooks.

"Raven tried his trick once too often. When Houskana, an expert fisherman, felt a tug, he jerked his line quickly, hooking something heavy. Raven pulled in the opposite direction. Then Raven grabbed hold of some rocks at the bottom of the ocean and called, 'O rocks, please help me!' But the rocks paid no attention. The fisherman pulled hard once again and Raven's beak broke off.

"Houskana pulled in his line immediately. There on the hook was a strange looking jaw. It scared the fishermen because they thought it might be an evil spirit. The fishermen picked up their gear and ran to their house as fast as they could.

"Raven came out of the water and followed the fishermen. Though he was in great pain for lack of his jaw, no one noticed his problem because he covered the lower part of his face with a blanket.

"The fishermen examined the jaw, handing it from one to another. Finally it was handed to the Raven who had changed into the shape of a man. He said, 'Oh, this is a wonder to behold!' as he threw back his blanket turned back into Raven and replaced his jaw.

"Raven performed his magic so quickly that no one had time to see what was happening. As soon as Raven's jaw was firmly in place again, he flew out through the smoke hole in the house. Only then did the fishermen begin to realize it was the trickster Raven who had stolen their bait and been hooked on Houskana's fishing line. But Raven was gone, having eaten all the fat the fishermen had prepared for fishing.

"Okay, time for bed children," said the grandfather.

"No. Just one more story!"

But the grandfather was tired and it was getting really late. The children reluctantly got up and walked to their beds with smiles on their faces.

The sun is creeping towards the horizon; I move back into our living room and talk with Joy for a while. "You know," I begin, "it is so interesting about the Trickster Raven. In the story of the fishermen, Raven is the third trickster in the story. The fat is the first trickster. Even though the fat doesn't know it he is lying to the fish, telling him he is a meal. But if the fish bites the fat, then the fish becomes the meal. The second trickster is the fisherman who is using the fat to trick the fish. The fat isn't really the meal, the fish is. And the third trickster is Raven who watches the fishermen cast their lines and then uses what the fishermen have taught him about baiting a hook to remove their bait from the hook. It is interesting that he gets caught and ends up paying the price of losing his beak only to trick the fishermen once again and fly away with his beak intact and a full stomach."

"Yes, I agree," Joy says. "But my favorite trickster story is the one where Raven eats all the berries. He starts out hungry and before long shows that he is a master of deception as he gets the crows to do his bidding and fill his belly. Creative deception has always been a prerequisite of art. It is in deception that art reveals truth. I think it was Aristotle who wrote about Homer saying, 'he taught the rest of us the art of framing lies the right way.' And it was the trickster god Hermes who invented lying when he was a child wanting meat."

"Yes, I see what you mean," I respond. "And one more thing, in both stories Trickster does what he often does, he makes his prey help him spring the traps against them. The crows gather the berries and the fishermen put the fat on the hook and show Raven how to do it. It is the hunger of both the fishermen and the crows that motivates them. But it is Raven who is fed. And yet the Raven, who is so cunning, is not sneaky enough. He is caught stealing berries by a small snail and ends up being punished. The trickster Raven is punished when stealing bait by losing his beak. But in this case he gets it back and flies away free."

Win some, lose some.

Our discussion winds down and we agree it is time to head back to our home in Boise. I put my thoughts aside, we pack up our stuff, and drive away from McCall.

CHAPTER FOUR: THE ARTIST AND THE RAVEN

I see myself as being in a chain that stretches way back to paintings on the rocks. To a certain degree I'm using different materials, but the statement is the same.

Rick Bartow, Native American Artist

Rick Bartow's eye is both singularly his and a gift of sight for the rest of us. He brings us a way of envisioning human experience that illuminates not only his own but ours as well. His often unsettling though richly beautiful imagery renders the invisible world of the spirit into the visible realm of the figurative. Bartow seems unafraid of exploring the most threatening of emotions: grief, terror, loss, great desire. Perhaps it is better to say that he is not afraid of exposing his own fear in the face of such powerful feelings. And while he has had his share of tragedy, his art is not so much about his struggles as a way through them.[7]

Back in Boise after our recent McCall visit, Joy tells me there is an artist who is having a showing at the Boise Art Museum. She asks if I would like to go with her. Several times a year she invites me to join her at the museum. Normally she ends up going with my cousin and I stay home with our Shih Tzu, "Yoda."

This time, however, for reasons I do not understand, I accept her invitation. I have no idea some of the artist's work focuses on ravens. It is to the artist, showing at the Boise Art Museum, we now turn.

The Native American artist, Rick Bartow, draws me inward, into thoughts and emotions visited at the lake in McCall. His art turns my thoughts to Native American Tradition and Raven. Captivated by his artistry, I examine anew the world and humankind's place in it. The mystery, magic, and magnificence of his work guide me to silence and stillness, especially his ravens pictured in bondage.

Raven in the Idaho woods, Joy's book cover art, and Rick Bartow's bundled raven lithographs, now framed and occupying a central place in our living room, cannot go unnoticed. Nor will "Absinthe Dream," a Rick Bartow drypoint, hanging conspicuously in our home with human and raven masks integrated into his self-portrait. My McCall days with ravens, Joy's art, and the insights of Rick Bartow have found a definitive place in my thought and mind.

[7] Rebecca J. Dobkins quoted in Rick Bartow's My Eye, University of Washington Press, Seattle, Washington. 2015. p. 15

A few days after Rick's showing at the Boise Art Museum we purchased two raven lithographs. Tonight I sit in my favorite old leather chair, sipping on a fine scotch while looking at Rick Bartow's art, mesmerized by the two acquired lithographs, "Red Raven Bundle" and "Blue Raven Bundle." One raven has black feathers with a tinge of white and is bound in a bright red shroud. The other has distinct white feather supplement with black and bound in a strong blue binding.

The Raven Bundles are the first professional art, or any art of quality other than Joy's that we have ever owned. Looking at them in the still and quiet of the evening I am lost in space not defined by time, as the great artist takes me to places inside myself I have rarely visited and never given more than cursory examination to the shadows he brings to light. I know I have to explore this unique artist to better understand his work as well as myself. Ignoring Rick Bartow is not an option. Forgetting about his forty-three inch tall Raven lithographs is not possible.

Being new to art appreciation, I try to pigeonhole Bartow's style of art and come up wanting. The late artist reached back into ancient myths, drew from a variety of cultures, and had interpretive insight into our contemporary environment. He blended historic tradition with his present experiences. Rick called his art "transformational images." His work, in all its complexity, sprang forth from Native American stories, experiences of both darkness and light, international exposure, academic learning, curiosity, and his love of people.

Charles Froelick, Rick Bartow's close friend and owner of the Froelick Gallery in Portland, Oregon, that represents Bartow's art, said, "(Rick is)….a conceptual artist; he tells stories through marks and images."

Rick told the writer, Raymond Carver, he wanted his art stories to be open and not impose "one truth" on the viewer. His art provides broad clues as to meaning, but details are vague and unspecified allowing for personal interpretation.

I now know it was this approach to art that drew me to the Wiyot Indian, Rick Bartow.

WIYOT HERITAGE

Wiyot Indians live in what is known today as Indian Island, near Eureka in Humboldt County, California. They settled at this location around 1850 and lived peacefully for several years with the white settlers nearby.

In 1858 the amicable relationships began to change. The settlers were letting their cattle stray onto Indian lands. The Wiyots treated the stray cattle as if they were their own and the cattle owners retaliated. By 1860 tensions had reached a fever pitch.

On February 26, 1860, around 6:00 a.m. most of the tribal men were away gathering supplies as part of continuing preparation for the World Renewal Ceremony that was held annually for as far back as anyone could remember. The ceremony was to focus on the healing of the earth, the tribe, families, and people everywhere. Through dance motions they would scoop the bad from the earth and bring down the Creator's good medicine and stomp it into Mother Earth with their dancing feet. The ceremony brought balance back into the world.

On that fateful winter morning it was mainly women, children, and the elderly who were home in the settlement.

Male residents from the town attacked the tribe.

Based on Wiyot Tribal estimates, somewhere between 80 and 250 Wiyot people were murdered. It is unknown if the attackers realized when planning the assault that most the men were away and the victims would be women, children, and older men. The massacre ensued with victims slain with knives and axes. Some shots were fired as well. There were very few survivors.

> Arcata's local newspaper, the *Northern Californian*, described the scene:
>
> *Blood stood in pools on all sides; the walls of the huts were stained and the grass colored red. Lying around were dead bodies of both sexes and all ages from the old man to the infant at the breast. Some had their head split in twain by axes, others beaten into jelly with clubs, others pierced or cut to pieces with the bowie knives. Some struck down as the mired; others had almost reached the water when overtaken and butchered.*

On February 28, 1860, approximately forty more Wiyot were killed on the South Fork of the Eel River. A few days later at Eagle Prairie thirty-five more tribal members were slaughtered. There was widespread condemnation of the hateful and primitive acts but no one was ever prosecuted for the murders.

Bret Harte wrote the following editorial and was forced to leave the area because of threats to his life that followed:

> *A More shocking and revolting spectacle was never exhibited to the eyes of a Christian and civilized people. Old women, wrinkled and decrepit, lay weltering in blood, their brains dashed out and dabbled with their long gray hair. Infants scarce a span long, lay with their faces cloven with hatchets and their bodies ghastly with wounds.*

As difficult as theses words are to read, they are shared here to describe the horror the Wiyot people experienced. Rick Bartow was born into the Wiyot culture eighty-six years later.

PERSONAL LIFE

Rick Bartow came into the world December 16, 1946. He was born in Newport, Oregon. His grandfather, John Bartow, had migrated on foot from Humboldt County to Oregon around 1911 and eventually ended up in Newport on the Oregon coast. One of John's six children, Richard, was Rick's father. Richard died when Rick was only five. Rick's Native American heritage, however, remained central in his life. When in Newport he visited a sweat lodge weekly. He was a member of the Mad River Band of the Wiyot Indians until his own death. He attended the Wiyot's World Renewal Ceremony in 2014, the first such ceremony held since 1859.

Following his father's death in 1951, Rick's mother, Mabel, who was of European decent, married Andrew Mekemson, who Rick thought of as his second father. Rick's Native American roots remained the central part of his essence for his entire life although his roots were supplemented by his mother's Christian background and his own international and historic exposure.

Rick was interested in art from the time he was a young child. He graduated from Western Oregon University in 1969 with a degree in art education. From college he went to Viet Nam (1969-1971) where he was awarded the Bronze Star. He was haunted by war and killing, bringing to the front of his mind the atrocities of his own experience as well as the suffering of his ancestors. The lack of value given life in the Viet Nam war was reminiscent of his learning a Wiyot skull could be purchased for four dollars. Life, loss, and the horrors of war guided Rick to alcohol. He became an alcoholic.

In 1979 he succeeded in breaking his bondage to the demon bottle. His art started to gain more color and hope than his earlier work. This is when Rick first called his expressionism "*transformational images.*"

ART AS TRANSFORMATIONAL

There are moments in our lives when we know we are transforming, when life's circumstances or events have changed us forever. We know we will never be the same again. For White Raven it was the time alone in the Great Northwest after killing his brother. For me it was the events surrounding my car accident, symbolized by the free spirit of ravens outside my hospital window.

One such moment for Rick Bartow was in 1999 when his wife, Julie Swan, was diagnosed with breast cancer and died a few months later. Rick would never be the same. For a year he "dropped out", unable to paint or think well. He had changed forever.

The moment of transformation is when we recognize we cannot go back to who we were before. Life as we know it has been shattered. Rick's art captures such transformation moments.

Accompanying such traumatic life changing events is the mandorla where life's contradictions and losses threaten to destroy us, while providing opportunity for new insight and new birth.

Bob Hicks, a culture writer, penned these words in the Oregonian in 2002:

The making of an artist—or any human being—is a careful balancing of contradictions, a reconciliation of things that don't fit. Bartow is an easy, generous, open man, and he has been in bleak places. He knows great joy and great sorrow. When the two resolve, they find a state of grace.

Through his "transformations" Rick maintained his traditional roots while allowing his personal experiences to move his expression forward. His art remained true to his Native American heritage, while the challenges life brought supplemented his art with inspiration from Japanese prints, the Maori of New Zealand, African art, and even a touch of ancient cave art.

Although Native American myth and legend were important to his artistic expressions, he did not try to retell traditional stories but rather used tradition as a means to show his personal transitions out of loss and addiction. Bartow said, "I'm an artist who happens to be Indian. I'm involved in what I can find in my culture, and I use that in my work. Wisdom is wisdom." The personal honesty and integrity in his art assists us in facing our own contradictions and losses while providing insight into our transformations.

It would be incorrect to label Rick Bartow a folk artist; however, it would be inaccurate to say folklore had no influence on his expressions. For example, shape-shifters, shared consciousness with animals, and Raven mythology, all speak to the influence of folklore in his work. The variety of traditions and historical cultures he called on provided him the icons through which to see and interpret his own life story. At the same time, Bartow's art sets the observer's mind ablaze, causing us to see ourselves through new eyes.

Near the end of his life, Bartow's work showed much more optimism than his earlier endeavors. His later artistic expressions, while still showing his struggles in life, are filled with light and, therefore, are more hopeful than his earlier work. His art is a mandorla revealing the power and insight that comes from blending the dark and light present in us all.

In a 2016 YouTube video, Bartow explained that he gave up drinking and drugs in 1979 but still struggled with the pain, fear, and depression of post-traumatic stress disorder that followed him since Viet Nam. Although tempered in later life, darkness and death were always part of Rick and, therefore, his art.

There were times when personal darkness overwhelmed Rick and could not be balanced by the light. In 1989 Rick wrote, "When I returned from Viet Nam, like so many others, I was a bit twisted. I was a house filled with irrational fears, beliefs, and symbols. Wind-blown paper would send me running, crows became many things; I never remembered dreams and detested the wind; I wore bells on my wrists so I could hear my parts when they moved; I slept in my clothes so I'd be ready to go nowhere at all. And I once recall answering when asked my name and where I was from, 'Nobody. Nowhere.' I must have been a wonderful companion."

Rick was always vulnerable, sharing his deepest emotions with friends and in his art. The events in his life, whether good or bad, brought new insights to his understanding of self and the world. He evolved out of his deep depressions and wrote, "Transitions are a part of my life that I now actively seek, seeing transition as growth." At other times he would recognize he was afraid of change. This contradiction resided inside Rick all his life.

In 1987 Bartow painted "Man in a Box." The subject of the painting has been beaten up and bound in a box. Bartow wrote, "When high hopes are lost I find myself feeling like that. A slash here and there and suddenly circumstances offer a new set of problems. There is a line from Alcoholics Anonymous that refers to man being 'in a box of space and time.' The man can't see anything outside the box but must trust that there is something." Bartow said.

"Man in the Box XII," 1987, artist Rick Bartow

His boxed man speaks to the struggle so many face. "Even in our most negative times we can survive our plight through personal struggle. I also heard the Native American Medicine Man Rolling Thunder speak of escape from the darkness into the light," Rick adds.

I sit in my living room thinking of one of my major transformations. When I left the ministry of the church, I was harshly judged by some, not all, family and friends. The immediate price of choosing freedom from a role that bound me was moving from a knight in shining armor to a dark horse with some beloved family members. In facing myself I gained insight into my own character and brought balance to my life. Over time most all my family has come to accept and respect the decision I made.

Being bound or bundled reveals internal trauma. Inner scars are made visible in Bartow's symbolic work, "The Man in a Box." The man can struggle, dance, or sit quietly as if in contemplation. The box binds its occupant within its walls, but neither ceiling nor floor is present in the painting, making escape possible.

As in all of Bartow's work, his meaning is personal, but the ultimate interpretation is left up to the viewer. It is valuable, however, to understand what the art means to the artist. Bartow gives us hints when he speaks of his own pain and darkness as well as that of Native Americans in general. He also leaves a way out of the box.

RAVEN IMAGES

Significant examples of how art expressed Rick's life experiences are found in his work with Ravens. In 1989 Rick wrote a revealing sentence: "My old nemesis, the crow (he used crow and raven interchangeably), took on a new twist. We became one while remaining two." Nine years later in 1998 Bartow commented on the familiar Northwest Native myth of the Raven and the sun box. A version of this legend is shared earlier in this book. The specific story Bartow refers to is called *Yealth* which is the Tlingit word for raven. In his painting "Crow Story" (see in My Eye) Bartow places a sun mask beside the crow, symbolizing his oneness with the great bird. The suns behind the Red and Blue Raven Bundle lithographs show this same oneness.

"Blue Raven Bundle," 2001/2005, artist Rick Bartow "Red Raven Bundle," 2001/2005, artist Rick Bartow

Rick Bartow on many occasions uses the "bundle" in his art to hold people or animals, especially ravens. His lithographs "Red Raven Bundle" and "Blue Raven Bundle" are prime examples of this. Rick wrote the following in reference to the "Man in the Box", but it applies to his raven bundles as well: "In certain Native American tribes there is a medicine rite in which a medicine man or medicine woman is bound in a quilt in the dark. It appears to me to be a binding of the physical body to release the spiritual body. In a successful ending of this ritual, the seeker is found free of the binding and the quilt." It was not unusual for Rick to acknowledge his personal oneness with Raven, and it can be concluded that for him his raven bundles represent the process of freeing his spiritual body.

In 2001, two years after his wife's untimely death, the Raven Bundles were being created at Rutgers University in New Jersey when September 11, 2001, changed us all. Rick ceased his work on the Raven Bundles and returned to Rutgers in 2005 to complete them.

While the bound ravens are not literally 'human', they do speak to people being bound in life, hint at the blending of human and animal life, and suggest the optimism that we can be set free. Man in a Box and the Raven Bundles, have no binding on the top or bottom of the works. The ravens' claws are beginning to show themselves near the top of the bundles. Bartow leaves a way out of bondage.

Bartow understood the mythical role of Raven, medium to and messenger from the Spirit World, creator of life, the world, beauty, and destroyer of what is loved. And as he knew all too well, life can trick you when you least expect it. And through it all, his oneness with the ravens remains.

One raven bundle was not enough to show the complete character of Raven. It took two, with one mainly black and the other having dominant white feathers. The two together are reminiscent of the myths and stories told earlier of white and black ravens.

INTERPRETING BARTOW

While Rick's work reveals part of himself, he does not feel obligated to share in detail what it reveals. We are left to interpret his art for ourselves. When people visit our Boise condo, where the raven lithographs are displayed, they invariably ask, "What do the ravens mean?" I always respond with the question, "What do you see in them?" The interpretations given to the bundled ravens are many and varied. Some see the raven as captive in the bundle, while others view the art as an expression of incubation, a time of silence and stillness, a time to pause and look inward. Others look at the lithographs, are turned off, and say things like: "It is nothing but a couple of birds in bandages, nothing to get excited about. The bird will suffer with his problems and die as a statistic. Nothing more." Fair enough.

If we choose to see only the physical, to live in a purely material universe, we cannot see magic in Bartow's work. There is no requirement saying we must think mystically. For many people myth needs no interpretation, they are just stories trying to explain how things got like they are in a fairytale sort of way. No one really believes folklore literally. Folklore is for entertainment purposes only. While such an interpretation of myth is prevalent, it misses the deeply personal interpretation others have.

Some observers see the raven bundles holding in abeyance the creative power of the great bird or keeping the trickster in tow. It can be seen as our struggles with personal trauma or the loss of a loved one while, paradoxically, offering hope and a way out. Several have noticed there is no binding at the top or bottom of the artwork. One person noticed a vaguely visible box around the Red Raven Bundle and an equally vague oval around the Blue Raven Bundle.

The person who framed our lithographs had suddenly lost her partner two years ago and found comfort in seeing the bundling as bandages that were healing the ravens. She was in the process of healing from the greatest loss in her life.

A family member looked at the lithographs and immediately responded: "I see humor. The trickster ravens were playing a game, cheated, and got caught up in their own deception. Those ravens deserve to be tied up in bundles. Won't they ever learn that playing fair keeps you from getting into such messes? Still, I must say, I love the Trickster in the raven." Another family member responded, "No, it looks like a raven in a papoose to me."

A friend suffering from physical disability that left him dependant on a walker to move from one place to another, used one word to describe the lithographs—"bondage." Then he took it a step further recognizing that the ravens' claws are sticking out of the top of the bundle providing hope that they would release themselves from bondage. My friend shared the hope of being freed from his bondage of the physical limitations that bind him in many ways, but not in all ways. I believe he had already freed himself mentally and spiritually. To keep such freedom is a daily challenge.

A seminary student looked long and hard at the lithographs and then shared the following thoughts: "The raven bundles are pictures of the crucifixion. The binding is the cross. The sun behind the ravens is the Spirit World shining through, as a halo does in Christian icons. The Creator is dying but may well free himself from the bundle. It is unclear why Raven is put in a bundle in the first place."

The seminarian continued, "The ravens just being there allows for all kinds of interpretation. Thoughts such as dying to return to a spiritual realm, giving life then allowing for its destruction, tricking us into loving and then taking it all away, can all be seen. The Raven of myth remains immortal, guiding, uplifting, providing comfort in time of need. And yet, the Raven tricks us with life's unpredictability. Sometimes the Spirit Raven is nowhere to be found during times of need. He is tied up somewhere. I love the Ravens in the bundles. They say without words so much about how I experience life."

From my perspective, there is a subtle message in the color of the raven bundles. The Sioux speak of "Red and Blue Days." The colored days are the progression to the end of time. At the end of days the moon will turn red and the sun blue. Red represents all that is sacred, especially that from which we come and to which we return. Blue is the color of the heavens. When a blue cover is placed upon the Sacred Pipe stem, which represents the earth, heaven and earth become united as one.

"Red and Blue Days" also refer to one's own life as it progresses towards death. There is an end to life as one has known it and rebirth into life anew. As in Christian baptism, there is death to old life and a new birth. Ego and ignorance die from life experiences and then are reborn with new insight and humility. In the days of red and blue, one experiences the guidance of the creator and gains new connections with the earth and all spiritual brothers and sisters including four-legged animals, winged life, finned, crawlers, and even plants and rocks.

My car accident is best interpreted as an experience of "Red and Blue Days." Following the wreck, I was reborn with a new appreciation for life. Questions I had never considered rose in my consciousness, and I was a new and different person. I fought to retain the familiarity of my old self, but to no avail.

A dry skin condition I had lived with since birth grew worse following the accident. Two years after the accident it was so bad I could not turn my neck from side to side. My skin resembled snake skin. That year, on Christmas vacation, I visited my parents. My mother, without asking me, set up an appointment with a dermatologist.

The nurse placed me in the dermatologist's office, not a regular examination room. I looked at all the plaques on the wall that revealed the dermatologist's life achievements, including the presidency of the American Academy of Dermatology.

He came into the room, didn't say anything, not even a greeting, held my chin in his hand, and looked at my neck. He was quiet for what seemed like forever. Then he spoke, "Hmmmm." He said no more but wrote out a prescription and threw it on his desk in front of me, got up and walked to the door. As he opened the door he turned and said his first words to me, "Oh, the prescription ointment will help some, but both you and I know that it won't solve the problem. Get your shit together." He then left, closing the door behind him. I never saw him again.

I knew what the dermatologist meant, and had known ever since by car accident. I needed to break out of my self-imposed binding. I needed to face myself honestly and put the mandorla of my life in balance. My rigid unbending attitude was making me an angry person. I had misused religion. It had become a hammer I referred to when making self-righteous points and judging others. The result was my serious skin condition. I was on a slippery slope the psychologist, Carl Jung, describes of moving from love, to justice, to judgment, to condemnation, to self-righteousness and rejection of the "other." It had to stop.

I could feel my attitude towards life changing as soon as I left the dermatologist's office. I retained my love for the spiritual questions religion raises concerning the mysteries of life. I just relaxed with my dogmatic and self-righteous answers.

Within a few months the skin problem was gone and has never returned.

Rick Bartow's bundles show there is a time to listen to the voice inside, the voice of the heart. Following the death of his wife, Rick was bound by loss and needed healing. Healing takes time. Rick went into his own wilderness, and, I believe, the blue and red bundles symbolized his healing process. The lithographs show the ravens beginning to break out of the bindings, having learned and matured from tragic loss, and using those insights to be "born anew."

Blue and red colors have also been used to symbolize great social change. For example, Black Elk tells the following story in Joseph Brown's book, The Sacred Pipe:

When the Lakota and the Ree people made peace between their tribes, the relationship was symbolized in a ceremony that mirrored the relationship of the Lakota with Wakan Tanka, the Great Spirit. The ceremony lasted several days. The women's faces were painted red and the men's red with a blue circle around the face and blues lines on the forehead, cheekbones and chin. The colors used on their faces symbolized they had been reborn and taken on new responsibilities and a new relationship. Past troubles between the two tribes are forgotten.

Another interpretation of the bundles is that they provide an incubation period where one is held perfectly still. The shaman uses stillness in his initial incubation period. The shaman goes through the initiation of a death experience, the ultimate stillness. It is stillness that brings him as close as possible to the divine world.

The ancient Greeks saw stillness in the same way. In fact, for the Greek philosophers it was only the divine that could be completely still. A common phrase in the Judeo-Christian tradition is "be still and know that I Am God."

In stillness the shaman encounters the riddle of life's meaning and while the shaman does not answer the riddle of being and life, he can enter the spiritual world and provide guidance and insight into the world we are all familiar with. He is a messenger from the Great Spirit and, often, especially in the Northwest, it is Raven who is the shaman's indispensible ally in making the journey to and from the Great Spirit.

FINE ART AND LIFE'S CHALLENGES

The word "mask" comes from the Latin word "persona" that means a concealing disguise. The persona is not a literal mask, rather it is all the social masks we wear depending upon the situation we are in. We use a mask to shield us from revealing ourselves.

Rick Bartow's home had masks on most every wall. He symbolically drew images with masks being removed or falling off his subjects on the canvas. The masks in his own life were revealed as he dealt with his alcohol and Viet Nam experiences. In his 2008 drypoint, "Absinthe Dreams," he has both human and raven masks drawn into a self-portrait.

Life can be difficult for each one of us, and masks can hide and protect us, keeping safe our vulnerable inner selves. We may mask our personalities in order to conform to social pressure or to cover inner emotions. Masks can cover many emotions such as anxiety, fear, sadness, anger, and embarrassment. Typical mask we ware to cover these emotions are amusement, boredom, contempt, happiness, or interest.

A major danger in mask wearing to conform to a situation or to cover our real feelings is that we may get lost in the process. We lose ourselves and becoming nothing but an extension of the thoughts and wills of those around us. "Absinthe Dream" reveals the personality and character of Rick Bartow who once was lost behind the mask of alcoholism. The red nose is symbolic of his excess drinking.

In "Absinthe Dream," like Bartow, we can all lose the focus of the main face by concentrating and getting lost in various masks. It is impossible to see Rick's self-portrait while focusing on the human and bird masks.

"Absinthe Dream," 2008, artist Rick Bartow

Rick described his own challenging experiences: "There are days when the studio or shop are my sanctuaries, there are days that they are sources of mental illness: anger, cursing, chairs kicked over/glass broken, paper torn and ripped; no tears come, only anger beyond the obvious. Then quiet jazz plays, Ute sings—a calm, a tide rip—a place between opposing currents…. The fear of the big failure subsides and while recalling the struggles the image resolves so that to my right eye and left eye it seems whole….and in making those fire filled marks, blind like John of the Cross I can find my way home through the darkness with my eyes closed." (Rick Bartow, 1989) The masks of Rick's self-described mental illness and anger melt away and he finds his true home, he honest self. The masks and his honest self blend expressing, through a mandorla, his creative genius.

Masks are not always negative. When a shaman dances with his ally's mask, such as a raven, he becomes one with the spirit of the mask and moves between the spirit and the physical worlds. The blending of the two realities provides insights that are otherwise unavailable.

Rick's art, when observed in silence and stillness, calls us to pause from learning by memorizing and absorbing other people's knowledge and to turn into ourselves. It is valuable to learn from others and esoterically analyze their observations and insights. That is a safe way to learn. As with the white raven turned black with his brother's blood, Rick's work calls the observer to look inward. It is not safe. We already have everything we need to examine the unexplored parts of ourselves. It is the longing for meaning that turns us from the outside to the inside, where we examine our darkness and find the hidden light. Sun, moon, and stars hang inside us, bringing light into darkness just as they bring light to the dark sky above.

THE LAST EXHIBITION

Following Rick's major and last stroke in 2013 he confessed, "After having suffered a stroke I had blind areas where birds flying across my visual field would simply vanish and I jokingly told friends that my head was filling with birds. Now with egg tempera, casein and gouache the birds are re-emerging from the tip of my brush, liberated in bold smears and dainty lines….It is with earth pigments that I am trying to portray the Spirit of the bird."

Rick's last exhibition went on tour throughout the United States beginning in 2015 and is continuing through 2019. The showing is titled, *Things You Know But Cannot Explain*. The German philosopher, Arthur Schopenhauer, coined the phrase in reference to "God who is whispering in man's ear in the background of one's life."

The title of Rick Bartow's showing describes the intuitive process that took place when Rick was painting, bringing together the physical and spiritual in a way that analytical thought and expression cannot. His art reveals the truth of our human condition. "Truth is truth," Rick used to say. Rick helped put together this last exhibition and was able to attend a few of its showings. He did not live to see the wonder in new visitors' eyes, mine included, as we encountered his work for the first time and found our own truths within it.

Rick Bartow died on April 2, 2016. His art is an autobiography.

He is generally acknowledged as one of the leading Native American artists of the twentieth and early twenty-first centuries.

The following are selected quotes from Rick Bartow as presented in the book, Things You Know But Cannot Explain, compiled by the Jordan Schnitzer Museum of Art:

"In the mark, in the chisel, you can't lie, you can't hide from it. Unless you don't do it at all."

"We have to reveal ourselves. In the way that we reveal ourselves, we let our life shine."

"There are old things which I have been able to lay my hands on. I've studied. I've listened. I sit by the truth. If you slow down a bit, you'll see that it will help you, too."

"Life experiences are not pleasant. They can scare the pee out of you!"

And finally, words repeated from earlier in this chapter:

"….and my old nemesis, the raven, took on a new twist. We became as one while remaining two."

Rick brings his age old tradition and his life experiences to our contemporary world. His ravens, emerging from myth and legend, speak to the moment. His personal tragedies bring creativity and honesty to his brush. Rick's ravens reveal his truth.

CHAPTER FIVE: RAVEN AND THE SHAMAN

Humans are part of creation and shamanism is our way of connecting with the whole.
Will Adcock

What people resist the most about spiritual healing is changing their minds.
S. Kelley Harrell

THE SHAMAN

In our scientific world where many educated thinking people have rejected spirituality because it cannot be observed or measured, it is difficult to accept the validity of shamanism. Shamanism is viewed as "voodoo" or part of primitive cultures and of little value today.

However, for those practicing shamanism it is understood not as a religion but a methodology. It is a methodology that takes us back to holistic approaches to health where the mind plays a major role. It is a methodology that recognizes our oneness with the earth and sees animals, plants, and all parts of the environment including soil, rocks, and water as our brothers and sisters. Shamans understand the power of life and death the earth holds over us. The shaman is equally at home in the field of the spiritual and the physical world.

The word "shaman" comes from the Sanskrit "sraman", meaning a worker or toiler. The shaman works on behalf of his or her people and toils in the field of the spiritual. He is a servant to his group even though he has special abilities and gifts. This ancient definition is supplemented by the Siberian definition of shaman which is "Skywalker." Together these definitions compile the working definition of a "skywalker" who toils in the fields of the spiritual on behalf of his people."

Wikipedia describes a shaman as one who reaches "altered states of consciousness in order to perceive and interact with a spirit world and channel these transcendental energies into this world." Shamans focus on such things as healing the sick, protecting the group from adversaries, and ensuring good hunting. He/she is a medium to the Spirit World with the help of an ally. One of the best allies a shaman can have is Raven.

Belief in shamanism is one of the oldest beliefs, dating back to the Paleolithic Period of the Stone Age (30,000 BCE-10,000 BCE). In some cultures shamans come from traditional lines of religious leaders while in other places the shaman is chosen by the spirits themselves. Whatever the genesis of becoming a shaman, the shaman always receives knowledge and wisdom directly from his or her spiritual allies. Spirits are around all the time, but shamans are in a unique and closer relationship to them than the regular member of a society.

RAVEN AS ALLY

For eons the rhythms of dance, drum, and rattle have brought forth the mysterious and all-encompassing presence and power of the spiritual world.

Shamanism, while not a religion, is based in the belief that people have a spiritual connection with spirits of animals, supernatural creatures, and all the elements of nature. A common thread in all shamanism is that the shaman receives knowledge and learns directly from the entity or entities who are his or her spiritual allies. These allies are generally secured at the time the shaman goes through a personal crisis or great illness and crosses over into the Spirit World and then is brought back to the physical world through the action of his/her allies. Most shamans have more than one ally with one being dominant.

The shaman's spiritual allies come in many forms, generally an animal or a bird. The ally's intercession and assistance with the Spirit World are essential to the shaman's success and integrity. Different parts of the world employ different allies normally indigenous to the environment.

The shaman and his Raven ally have played central roles in the myths and legends of the Great Northwest. As we have seen, tales of the Raven have pervaded the Indian culture. The blending of the human and animal psyches is fundamental to the Northwest Indian culture and to shamanism. Through power animal(s) the shaman connects with the power of the animal world and uses an animal as a power giving guardian spirit. In the Northwest United States the rattle is often in the shape of the Raven and the drum may have Raven painted on its skin.

The shaman uses dancing, drumming, and rattling to summon animal spirits. A shaman often wears a mask picturing his ally. The repeating rhythm takes the shaman into a frenzied condition in which the shaman produces the movements and cries of his ally. He is transported into an altered state of consciousness by the dancing, drumming, and rattling. The high pitched rattling takes the shaman to a deeper place than drumming alone does. The shaman becomes for a time the actual embodiment of the spirit residing in the mask. As one coastal Salish shaman said, "When you dance don't act, just follow your power ally." It is more than the animal spirit communicating with the shaman; the shaman is transformed into the animal. Their spirits are now one.

The shaman dances shaking the raven rattle with its beak pointing down. When using the rattle in dance the shaman/raven ally is the medium of the Great Spirit to the people and the earth, hence, the rattle points down from the Spirit World to the earth. In dance the Great Spirit is stomped into the earth, healing it. In addition, a rattle like the one shown below, is used to channel the raven ally as the shaman's spirit guide and is used in healing ceremonies. The use of the rattle transmits the power of the raven to humankind. Rattles are very personal and powerful and a shaman uses a rattle carved into the shape of his ally.

Raven rattle/Native American (Tsimshian) Courtesy of Metropolitan Art Museum, New York.

Raven is as powerful an ally as there is in the shamans' world. Shamans were among the first people in various parts of the world to recognize the special role of Raven. From Siberia down through the Northwest United States, a shaman is considered fortunate to have Raven as an ally. This smartest of all birds can uniquely cross between the world of the living and the dead.

The shaman understands there are good spirits and bad spirits. It is the bad spirits that cause all the trouble, suffering, sickness, and death. The shaman has knowledge of the spirits and access to the spirit world through his ally. He knows the strength of both the bad and good spirits, the important role they all play in knowing ourselves and finding life's balance, and the strength spirits have in both healing and destroying. The shaman, becoming one with his Raven ally, enters the spirit world. The shaman with Raven ally brings to the tribe and individuals balance, homeostasis, and healing.

The Shaman uses a variety of practices to communicate with the spiritual world when the tribe is facing adversity or needs to obtain solutions to problems afflicting the community or individuals, including sickness. The shaman's ally, Raven, facilitates this as a medium riding the wind of "holy smoke" to the Other World. Raven and shaman have become one and travel the RavenWind to communicate with the Great Spirit.

A shaman understands that what the physical eye sees may not always be the whole truth, and he calls upon Raven to bring clarity or healing to a situation. In visiting the spirit world, the shaman relies on Raven to act as guide, mediator, or messenger from the Spirit World to the material world. As the shaman becomes the Raven spirit, healing power and wisdom from the Great Spirit are received and taken to the material world, where the shaman puts torn lives back together and heals the wounds, both physical and spiritual, of individuals and the community.

THE SACRED PIPE

Unique to the North American continent is the use of the sacred pipe which is normally generated by the shaman or tribal chief.

Between 200B.C.—A.D.500 the Hopewell culture flourished along the rivers in the Northeastern and Midwestern United States. They built ceremonial structures in which burial rites were performed. All kinds of sacred objects, especially pipes, have been found in the ruins. The Hopewell culture was not a single society but many diverse groups that were connected by a shared network of trade routes. It is probable these were the original pipe smokers.

Initiated by Hopewell, the use of a sacred pipe spread across the continent. Shamans use a sacred pipe in ceremonial events to honor Spirits of the past and the future and to ask blessings for peace in the universe.

The pipe holds the living breath of the Great Spirit. Smoke coming from the mouth is truth spoken; smoke rising in the air provides a path to reach the Great Mysterious Spirit.

The pipe is used only as a spiritual artifact, never for personal pleasure or amusement. The sacred ceremony is simple. The pipe is filled with tobacco often supplemented with sweet smelling herbs, and local barks and roots. The growing of the tobacco is the sacred responsibility of the "Tobacco Society" of the tribe. Specific tobacco growing techniques vary from tribe to tribe.

Typically the smoke is not inhaled. Rather it is puffed in and out of the mouth four times facing the four directions on earth and recognizing the sacred in all directions. The sacred pipe ceremony acknowledges Father Sky, Mother Earth, and the Great Spirit. The pipe is passed from person to person around a circle.

It is not unusual for the sacred pipe bowl to be in the shape of a raven because of Raven's role as messenger and mediator to the Great Spirit. To this day, Raven Ceremonial Pipes are made of solid sacred red clay called pipestone by the fifth generation Oglala Lakota pipe maker, Alan Monroe. The special red clay pipestone called Catlinite is mined only from the Pipestone National Monument in Pipestone, Minnesota.

The raven shaped bowel is made of Catlinite from the Pipestone National Monument. Photo courtesy of Crazy Crow Trading Post, the world's largest source of Native American craft supplies.

The sacred significance the pipestone has for a specific tribe is found in a Lakota Sioux legend:

In times long past there was a great flood. The people and buffalo climbed up a mountain to save themselves. The water kept rising and the people continued to climb higher. They reached the top of the mountain but the water kept rising and the people and buffalo perished. As the waters retreated the blood of the people and the buffalo gathered in one pool and solidified creating a quarry of pipestone. That is why the pipe is made of pipestone red clay from the sacred quarry. It is made with the blood of ancestors.

The red bowl is the flesh and blood of ancestors, its stem is the backbone of the people long dead, and the smoke rising from the bowl is their breath, their spirit. The chanunpa (pipe) comes alive when it is used in a ceremony and the power of ancestors flowing from it is felt by the participants.

SACRED DANCE AND CHANTS

Hundreds of years ago in the Northwest shamans would use dance to become one with a "power animal" or "guardian Indian" as the allies were called. The shaman finds the spirit guardian in the tempo, movements, and animal gestures in the dance. Along the Northwest Coast the dancers often used masks and claws to bring forth the guardian spirit. Raven is the dominant and most prestigious ally on the Northwest Coast.

Dance with the rhythm of the drums and rattles is often used in conjunction with the holy smoke. This sacred ritual places the shaman in a space where he can call on his ally to mediate with the Great Spirit on behalf of the people. The shaman enters a trance where the sound and movement used in repetition draw the shaman into another world with his ally. The ally guides the shaman on the smoke path to the Great Spirit.

Shamans know protective words and chants that disarm bad spirits and call forth the good spirits. The shaman uses the words and chants in healing ceremonies. Knowledge of the words and chants and the ability to use them is called "medicine" and it is steeped in mystery. The "medicine" comes from the Great Spirit and is spoken by the shaman. Words and chants are carried on the breath that forms them. Hence, the shaman using sacred wind or breath is called a medicine man or man of mystery.

The shamanistic medicine works in the context of four major categories: 1) spirituality (Creator, Mother Earth, Great Father); 2) community (family, clan, tribe/nation); 3) environment (daily life, nature, balance); and 4) self (inner passions and peace, thoughts, and values).

The Shamanistic oneness with animals is a timeless worldwide phenomenon. Ancient shamans in Western Europe were known to transform themselves into animals. In 1558 the scientist and alchemist, Giovanni Battista Porta, described in his famous book, Natural Magick, the formula for metamorphosing into an animal. Drums, rattles, and dance were keys to a transformation into an animal. The book was so popular it was translated into several languages. It's most recent publication was in 2005 by NuVision Publications.

THE JON TURK STORY

When Native American people emigrated from Siberia to what would later become the United States, they brought with them the ancient tradition of shamanism. As communities were established in the new land much Siberian belief and tradition were retained. All life was part of the same cosmology, the same spirit, and of equal value in the minds and emotions of these ancient people.

Jon Turk, an adventurer and writer for National Geographic, tells of his experience in Siberia with an old woman shaman and her Raven ally. The sacred bird Jon Turk writes about in his book, The Raven's Gift, is essential to make contact between the world of spirit and the world of the physical.

While traveling in Siberia, Jon Turk meets an old woman in her nineties by the name of Moolynaut. Moolynaut is a shaman. Her ally and spiritual guide is Raven, called *Kutcha*. She cannot do her work of healing Turk from a serious physical problem without the help of *Kutcha*; however, she says to Turk: "Kutcha is only a messenger god. He is not the highest God. Our highest God is the whole tundra. You must understand that God lives in every rock, lichen, and sedge."

In time Moolynaut, with Kutcha's assistance in a ceremony, heals Turk's cracked pelvis, a serious problem that was affecting his ability to explore.

One day the old woman asks Turk to go into the great tundra. After stalling for some time, he finally consents to the shaman's pressure for him to embark on a perilous journey to thank the Great Spirit, Tundra, for his healing. Moolynaut says to Turk before he leaves, "You are a poor traveler in the Other World....You must make a long, hard journey...in the Real World. You will be hungry and tired. Then maybe, if you are lucky, you will find what you are looking for."

Turk goes into the tundra to thank the Great Spirit. He writes: "If you take the time to seek, believe in, hold on to, and appreciate the magic that surrounds us, all the time, you would be a lot better off than if you passed the Magic Mountains of your life without taking a moment to touch—and be touched by—them."

At the beginning of his wandering in the great tundra, Turk wondered why he was there. Then, after a month of traveling, he saw it. Raven flying towards him from a distance, flying purposely towards him. The great bird arrived, paused, looked down and calked his head as if to say, "Hello down there. Thank you for coming." He flew closer and they looked each other in the eye.

Turk writes: "Such a tiny head, such a tiny brain," I thought. "How can it fly, eat, make love, care for its young, have friends, lie, cheat, share, even fabricate tools, with such a tiny brain? It cawed once, twice, three times...acknowledging me. I felt accepted...and then he flew away."

In the tundra Jon Turk's life had a transformational moment. He experienced the Great Spirit and realized he was part of a wonderful and mysterious universe.

Now back in his Montana home, Jon Turk and his wife Chris looked forward to skiing as often as possible. On a beautiful day turned tragic, they met skiing friends, and headed to the slopes. Skiing down the mountain, Chris was swallowed up by not one but two avalanches. She did not survive.

Jon grieved deeply, while at the same time knowing he needed to continue living. But how to make such a transition? With loss was so great, continuing on seemed impossible.

Jon planned a memorial for Chris. After the memorial, Chris's sister Karen and Jon took Chris's ashes into the high British Columbia mountains. After walking for hours they saw in the distance, a raven. Could this be *Kutcha*, who hovered over him in the tundra and had gone to the Other Word for Moolynaut to heal Jon's pelvis?

Jon watched as the great bird dived into the canyon. He felt himself swoop down the mountain on the wind of *Kutcha* and Chris's spirit, whose ashes he held in his hand.

Karen, who had separated from him, soon caught up, asking Jon if he too had seen the beautiful raven gliding down the canyon.

They finished the climb to the summit, opened the urn, and allowed Chris's ashes to join the wind. The ashes swirled in the sky sharing the gentle wind with Raven. Chris continues the mysterious journey we all take. And Jon found peace.

Lest it be thought Jon Turk is some kind of new age weirdo, it must be added that he was initially a research chemist probing into the nature of chemical bonds that hold all matter together. He left becoming an adventurer and in 2012 was a National Geographic top ten adventurer. His adventures in Siberia introduced him to the shamanic world and changed his life forever. He does not try to explain how the old shaman and *Kutcha* healed his pelvis, he just knows they succeeded where other doctors had failed.

I do not go out on my deck this late August morning, but stay inside, looking through the sliding glass window at the early morning fog gliding across the silent still water. And yes, my mug and I are sharing a cup of coffee.

I know the shaman is onto something. It is hard to be content with merely living life until we give out physically and die. We need more. We seek the sacred in our lives.

For thousands of years shamans and the Raven ally have brought the spiritual "medicine" of healing to people. The shaman can bring mysterious richness in the midst of suffering and purposeful direction in the midst of ambiguity. No doubt, I think to myself, the shaman has brought the power of the unseen, the experience of the other world, and the indwelling of the Spirit to countless lives across the world and over the centuries.

And yet for many, "spiritual" can be evasive and even difficult to describe. One can look and never find the "indwelling of the spirit."

Arguably the greatest poem ever written on American soil exposes the loneliness and pain of loss when one has searched in vain but has not found the "spiritual."

The fog lifts, I pack my suitcase and head back to Boise with Edgar Allan Poe's great poem running through my mind.

CHAPTER SIX: RAVEN, DARKNESS, AND EDGAR ALLAN POE

Once upon a midnight dreary, while I
pondered weak and weary,
Over many a quaint and curious volume
of forgotten lore—
While I nodded, nearly napping,
suddenly there came a tapping,
As of some one gently rapping, rapping
at my chamber door—
Only this and nothing more.
The Raven, by Edgar Allan Poe

Open here I flung the shutter,
when, with many a flirt and flutter,
in there stepped a stately raven,
of saintly days of yore.
Nor the least obeisance made he;
not a minute stopped or stayed he;
But with mien lord or lady,
perched above my chamber door."
The Raven, by Edgar Allan Poe

Ghastly grim and ancient Raven wandering from the Nightly shore—
Tell me what thy lordly name is on the
Night's Plutonian shore!
Quoth the Raven, "Nevermore."
The Raven, by Edgar Allan Poe

Poe published his first book, Tamerlane and Other Poems, in 1827. He was the editor of the *Messenger* in Richmond, Virginia, from 1835-1837. In the late 1830s he published The Fall of the House of Usher. In 1841 he initiated a new genre of detective fiction with The Murders in the Rue Morgue. To this day he is known as the "father of the detective story." *The Raven* was first printed on January 29, 1845, in the New York Evening Mirror.

The Raven was an instant hit, making Edgar Allan Poe a household name. Unfortunately, the poem did not solve his lifelong struggle with poverty. Poe said, "I have made no money. I am as poor now as ever I was in my life, except in hope, which is by no means bankable." He was paid nine dollars for *The Raven.*

While driving back to Boise, I reflect that as a fourteen year old, I thought Poe's Raven was "groovy." I liked it so much that when my eighth grade English teacher required us to pick a poem and write about its poet, I chose Edgar Alan Poe and "The Raven."

The way the poem flowed fascinated me. The Raven, appeared out of nowhere, gave Lenore's lover no hope to restore the past, and impressed me with its rare honesty.

I felt a kinship with Poe even as a young teenager. I feared death, and appreciated the way Poe addressed the subject head on. I knew he shared my fear. We also shared a lack of money. I was always broke and so was he. I was mowing lawns for fifty cents a yard. Neither Poe nor I possessed great business minds.

I wondered why a wise talking raven didn't seem strange. Poe first thought the bird in his poem should be a parrot, because a parrot knew how to talk. But a parrot would be inappropriate for the poem. The ambiance of a parrot just wasn't right.

The raven was a bird of mythology, used by shamans and kings, and instilled mystery and a touch of fear in his observers. Mythology made him an eternal messenger from the gods. Raven was a perfect fit for the poem.

I recently learned my father loved Edgar Allan Poe, and in particular "The Raven." He memorized the iconic poem. For years he would recite it at service clubs, church groups, and other organizations. He would share some of Poe's life, and respond to questions. Memorizing the poem helped him with his memory which he feared was slipping prior to his death in 1995. I am curious, but do not know, why both my father and I were drawn to The Raven.

I have been home for a couple of days. It is the last day of August 2018, and a beautiful evening here in Boise as I think of childhood, my father, and Edgar Allan Poe. I sit in my old leather chair, sipping a newly discovered twelve year old single malt scotch from a distillery established in 1815 on the Isle of Islay, Scotland. It bears the name Ardbeg. Edgar Allan Poe was only six years old when Ardbeg was first introduced. I wonder if he ever sipped or drank to excess this fine scotch whiskey.

I watch as the setting sun changes the colors of the ancient foothills north of Boise. As a young boy I played in those foothills, finding arrowheads from time to time. This land I love is still possesses my childhood emotions as well as the long forgotten memories of the Shoshone Indians who lived, loved, laughed, fought, and died here. The raven's caw remains even to this day.

I reach to my bookshelf and pick a book containing Poe's masterpiece, "The Raven." In now, my last stage of life, I once again revisit Poe's bird of "lore." Over time, my perspective on the poem has changed.

The reason I returned from McCall a few days ago was to conduct the funeral service for a close friend of forty years, Bob.

Quote the Raven, 'Nevermore.' I read the familiar words as if for the first time, pause, sip the scotch, and put down the book. The silent darkness around me will never again be broken by Bob's laughter. Memories once shared, now mine alone. "Nevermore," quoth the raven, "Nevermore." The words speak to me in ways that were not possible when I was a young boy. The questions surrounding life and death grow as my personal time diminishes.

THE POEM

Poe writes, "In there stepped a stately raven, of saintly days of yore." As "stately," Raven brings a royal countenance and no "obeisance", which is a friendly greeting. The raven offers no cure for the loss of Lenore. When the sufferer in the poem asked, "Tell me…is there balm in Gilead?" (The "Balm in Gilead" is referenced from the Old Testament where it is a spiritual medicine able to heal Israel.) The Raven's only reply was, "Nevermore." The word means that nothing will ever again be as it was. The life of the young man and the love of Lenore he held so dearly are gone forever.

This is not your run of the mill raven. It is Raven with a capital "R" that we see in Native American and other mythology. Poe's Raven comes from older, nobler times of the "saintly days of yore", meaning Raven is not bound by time or space but has a mystical mysterious quality from the Otherworld. Raven is the intermediary between the material and spirit worlds, much as he is in Native American folklore. Poe does not question Raven as he sits above the "chamber door." Poe does not ask to see Raven's credentials or challenge his eternal knowledge.

"Perched upon a bust of Pallas just above my chamber door—Perched, and sat, and nothing more." Poe, well versed in Greek mythology, places the stately Raven on the "bust" of the Greek goddess Pallas, who is also known as Athena, the Greek goddess of Wisdom.

When asked, Poe would say, the Raven in the story represented the messenger from the afterlife. The bird was symbolic of spirit and, paradoxically, mortality. Both understandings are found in Greek and other mythologies as well as in Indian folklore. Raven speaks the language of people, binding together the human and animal worlds. All are of one spirit. And, as we have discussed, the same bird could be found eating fallen soldiers on the battle field, emphasizing man's finitude. Raven comes from the Great Spirit, the Great Mystery, but offers no relief for the pain of loss on earth.

There is no explanation of Raven's beginning, why he has so much knowledge of life and death, or how he is able to talk. As in Native American mythology, Raven just is. Perched upon the bust of Pallas, his wisdom comes from the gods.

The devastated young man in the poem drifts from exhaustion and deep grief into madness. This process is led by the Raven, who is both mysterious and prophetic.

Poe seeks the return of his relationship with Lenore. It is not found. Even his immortal soul is changed forever. He ends the poem with the words: "And the Raven, never flitting, still is sitting, still is sitting on the pallid bust of Pallas just above my chamber door; and his eyes have all the seeing of a demon's that is dreaming, and the lamp-light o'er him streaming throws his shadow on the floor; and my soul from out that shadow that lies floating on the floor shall be lifted—nevermore."

The haunting poem has touched countless lives for more than 170 years. The Raven brings up dark feelings from the depth of my psyche. It forces the power of loss to the front of my mind. I experience the sorrows life has brought, while offering no way to retrieve that which is lost. And still, there is recognition of the Great Spirit, the Great Mystery, from whence the Raven comes. Unlike Lenore's lover, I am not driven into madness. For me, the Raven offers hope and fullness of life.

I take my empty scotch glass into the kitchen and go to bed.

THE LIFE OF EDGAR ALLAN POE

Poe was the son of itinerant actors and orphaned at age three. His father abandoned the home and his mother died soon after. Soon after being orphaned Poe was adopted by the wealthy tobacco merchant, John Allan, and his wife Frances.

John Allan wanted Edgar to follow in his footsteps and when he didn't, John disowned him. When Edgar went to the University of Virginia in 1826, where he excelled, John Allan sent only tokens of financial support. In 1829 Frances Allan died of tuberculosis. Shortly after Frances's death, Poe was accepted into West Point. He was kicked out after one year for failing to "handle his duties." His grades were fine.

When John Allan died in 1834, Poe believed his financial worries were behind him. Allan had an estate consisting of eight homes and shares in banks and gold mines. Poe's optimism was short-lived. He received nothing.

One of Poe's best paying jobs was at the *Messenger* in Richmond, Virginia, where he was editor. Although the position paid $520 a year, he missed his beloved wife in Baltimore. Poe was miserable and turned to drink.

An office boy at the *Messenger* said, “Mr. Poe was a fine gentleman when he was sober. But when he was drinking he was about one of the most disagreeable men I have ever met.” Drinking was considered a moral failure in the nineteenth century. When he would acknowledge his drinking, which was rare, he would call it his “illness.”

Paradoxically, Poe had a quiet charisma coupled with a beautiful voice and the intellect of a genius. Generally, he was a quiet and orderly man. Physically, he was handsome and an accomplished boxer, runner, and swimmer. As an adult he was a welcome house guest, the center of attention.

Poe’s writing delved into black mysteries—exposing the darker side of the emerging American psyche. He was fascinated by the occult, the mysteries of life and the terrors of death. The possibility of life after death dominated much of his thinking.

His literary acclaim, however, was never acceptable to rich society which was judgmental of his personal habits, the topics he explored in his writing, and his lack of financial resources. His enemies in the literary community were many and judged harshly both his work and lifestyle.

He was said to be an alcoholic, although this was disputed by those close to him. The stories of his drinking followed him long past his death, even until today. Most evidence points to Poe as a heavy drinker. He would drink when anxious or depressed. Like his father, when drinking he was moody and argumentative.

While Poe never uses the word “mandorla,” he certainly describes and lives the concept. Poe is a contradictory spirit confined (bundled) by his realities of poverty, despite the wealth of his foster parents. He was a genius struggling with the finality of death and the immortality of the soul. He could be sensitive or cold, loving or rejecting, accepting or unforgiving. His writing, as his life, struggled between opposites: creation/destruction, relationships/loneliness, and hope/despair. While the opposites gave insight and creativity to his writing, Poe the man never gained the balance he craved in his personal life.

In the midst of his tormented life, he loved women, especially his wife Virginia, who was his cousin and whom he married when he was twenty-six and Virginia was thirteen. Virginia became very ill with tuberculosis, suffering uncontrollable chills and terrible fevers. Poe was always there for her, an attentive and loving caregiver. Virginia died in 1847, at the age of twenty-four, with her husband at her side. This was the same age that Poe’s mother and brother died.

Poe never recovered from Virginia’s death. This major personal loss, coupled with poverty and some heavy drinking, were instrumental in Poe’s inability to keep his life in balance until his own death.

On February 3, 1848, The New York Tribune announced an upcoming lecture on *Mesmerism, Somnambulism, Clairvoyance and Hallucination*. It read: “Edgar A. Poe will lecture at the Society Library on Thursday evening, the 3d inst. At half-past 7. Subject, ‘The Universe.’ Tickets 50 cents—to be had at the door.”

A small group of sixty attended the lecture, witnessing a thin pale Poe speaking of the planets, gravitation and electricity. He spoke of the beginning and end of the universe, and of God. Poe continued his boring and embarrassing lecture by reading from a letter written in the future, the year 2848. Poe finished his presentation by requesting money to fund his *Stylus* magazine. Few contributions were forthcoming.

Poe printed 500 (he wanted to print 50,000) copies of *Eureka: A Prose Poem,* that he had based his lecture on. It is easily his most eccentric and confusing work. As his lecture, the written "Eureka" was a rambling, undocumented treatise on the cosmology. In his book Poe sees the material world coming forth out of the mind of the spiritual. He cannot define the spiritual because "it is greater than a person's brain."

"I design to speak of the Physical, Metaphysical and Mathematical," he wrote in Eureka, "of Material and Spiritual Universe—of its Evidence, its Origin, and Creation, its Present Condition and its Destiny."

He considered "Eureka" his greatest and most important work, saying it was more significant than the discovery of gravity. This was not the opinion of his critics; however, it must be added, some of Poe's ideas anticipate 20th century science, such as the controversial theory that consciousness is outside time and preceded the material universe.

Poe's 500 copies of "Eureka" did not sell well, nor did his magazine, "The Stylus." A year after the failed lecture, Edgar Allan Poe was dead. October 7, 1849. Age 40.

In September 1849 Poe was headed to New York to help a friend with her manuscripts. For unknown reasons he ended up in Baltimore. On October 3, he was found on the street outside a polling station. He was speaking incoherently in a semi-conscious state. He was taken to a hospital. Poe was wearing clothes that were obviously not his. He kept saying the name "Reynolds." His clothing and the name "Reynolds" have never been adequately explained. Poe lingered in the hospital for four days and then died. His last words were, "Lord help my poor soul."

The cause of Poe's death remains vague and disputed. It is surmised that Poe's death could have been caused by alcohol, murder, cholera, hypoglycemia, rabies, syphilis, influenza, or cooping. Even the Smithsonian is uncertain, saying the author may have succumbed to a brain tumor.

The confusion surrounding his last days led to the conclusion that his death was a mystery. Poe's obituary, filled with falsehoods and contradictions, contributed to his mythic legacy. His death is the stuff of folklore, of storytelling and legend. If anyone was worthy of such a mysterious death, it was Edgar Allan Poe.

AFTER POE'S DEATH

Poe's fame was international following the publication of *The Raven.* After his death, his fame faltered. His enemies, despising Poe, fanned the flames of deception and lies about him. His unreasonable critics were later described as "asses kicking at a dead lion." They painted his personal life with such dark colors, believed by the populous, that Poe soon became a forgotten man. The worst of his detractors was Rufus W. Griswald.

Rufus W. Griswald (1815-1857), a literary critic, writer, and poet had a personal and professional rivalry with Edgar Allan Poe. They both competed for the attention of poet Frances Sargent Osgood. Griswold did not like Poe and often demonstrated jealousy over Poe's literary success. Griswald followed Poe as the editor of *Graham Magazine* and received a higher salary than Poe, increasing tensions between the two.

Unfortunately, following Poe's death, Griswald wrote the first and, therefore, definitive biography of his life. The biography dominated the public understanding of Poe's life for the first twenty-five years after his death. It was full of lies, dark stories, and slander.

A weakness in human nature makes it easier for us to listen with pleasure to derogatory stories about others rather than to praise. It is much easier to start falsehoods than to stop them. Without analysis, Griswald's biography was accepted as truth. His biography evolved into negative folklore, circulating as untrue stories and false legends characterizing Poe as a drunken vagabond and literary plagiarist.

While Griswald's biography was later rejected, some of his falsehoods still appear in recent biographies. Then there are some biographies that throw the pendulum too far the other way, making Poe a saint without fault. The truth lies between the extremes.

Poe's gravesite was unknown for several years after his death. It took a quarter of a century for a stone to mark his place of burial. At one point Edgar Allan Poe's cousin, Neilson Poe, ordered a headstone. A folktale surfaced saying a locomotive crashed into the stonemason's studio and smashed the headstone to pieces. In fact, the headstone was destroyed by falling off a shelf. A new headstone was not made at that time.

Fortunately, in 1865 a group of "schoolma'ams" started collecting money to purchase a suitable headstone for the great writer. After a decade of collecting pennies, they had their monument. Poe's remains were moved to a prominent spot in the church graveyard and a monument put in place on a chilly November day in 1875. Over a thousand people attended the ceremony.

When Henry Wadsworth Longfellow was asked for an appropriate inscription for Poe's new monument he suggested the last two lines of Poe's famous poem *To Annie*

The poem in its entirety:

Thank Heaven! the crisis—
The danger is past,
And the lingering illness,
Is over at last—
And the Fever called 'Living'
Is conquer'd at last.

The popular poem was not placed on the grave stone.

In 1913 a gravestone was erected for the original site of Poe's grave, but it was not placed in the correct location. In 1921 it was moved to its present and right place.

Beginning in 1934 in the city of Baltimore and every year for seventy-five years, before dawn on January 19, a mysterious visitor, dressed in black, face hidden by scarf and hat, came to a particular gravesite in one of the city's cemeteries. The solemn figure raised a glass of cognac and toasted the grave and its former resident. The visitor would leave a bottle of cognac behind, accompanied by three roses. This still unknown figure would disappear into the dark, only to return a year later with a toast and a new bottle of cognac. The ritual ended in 2009 but was revised in 2017 by a new group of toasters.

Respect is still given to the occupant of the grave, a man born over 200 years ago on January 19, 1809, and dying under mysterious circumstances. During Poe's lifetime love was hard to come by and impossible to sustain. Ironically, centuries later he is loved and respected. His life, remembered and celebrated each year, has all the earmarks of legend. Edgar Allan Poe has cemented his place in the fine art of great poetry and in the lives of many of us. His Raven will live forevermore.

CHAPTER SEVEN: RAVENWIND

Isn't it a strange thing that we understand least of all what we know best of all, or rather: we know best of all what we do not understand at all, our soul, and, one may say, God.

Leo Tolstoy's diary dated July 1, 1910

Listen to the wind, it talks.
Listen to the silence, it speaks.
Listen to your heart, it knows.

Native American Proverb

O ancient rocks, Tunkayatakapaka, you are now here with us, Wakan-Tanka has made the Earth, and has placed you next to Her. Upon you the generations will walk, and their steps shall not falter! O Rocks, you have neither eyes, nor mouth, nor limbs; you do not move, but by receiving your sacred breath (the steam), our people will be long-winded as they walk the path of life; your breath is the very breath of life.

Black Elk

There are "things you know but cannot explain." Not everything is as it appears.

In traveling the Northwest and Southwest of the United States I experience the mysterious but real power that dwells within nature. Walking ancient trails, magical moments leave time behind and fill my soul with the spirit of the wind. I shed my body and fly over and within the mountains and rivers, contemplating sticks, small rocks, butterflies, birds, chipmunks, and the grandeur of it all. The physical world, no longer inanimate, pulsates with life. I enter the mystical world of Raven, not a world just of peace and quiet but conflict, drama, and forceful action as well. It is here I know myself best. It is here I challenge my beliefs, examine the shadows in my life, and gain insight for days ahead.

Early September, 2018, four months after my initial McCall lakefront experience with Raven, I sit on the Payette Lake beach in McCall, relaxing on a white plastic chair shaded by an inadequate off-white umbrella stuck in the middle hole of an unstable table. The lake sand is beautiful, warm, and inviting. It is Indian summer, my favorite time of year.

I brought to the beach a tuna sandwich and chips for later consumption. Taking a sip of coffee from the ever present coffee mug, I say, "We have been through a lot together, haven't we old friend?" The mug responds with silence. "At least Yoda wags his tail when I talk to him," I say with emphasis.

This treasured mug was a gift from my friend Ted who provided opportunity for me to teach long term care providers around the world. I received the mug when healing from a bout with colon cancer in 1998, a few years before Ted's death.

I close my eyes and think of my friend as a warm breeze blows over, around and through me. Grief, fifteen years later, sometimes managed, sometimes not, remains. "Talk to me," I request again of my terra cotta companion. Nothing. An unseen raven's distant "caw" is barely audible. I believe part of Ted's spirit resides in the mug.

I sit in silence, on the verge of sleep, eyes heavy from the sun's warmth. I take a deep breath as my eyes close.

Unsolicited, I hear a whisper in my mind, "Yes, we have been through much."

"Huh? Is that you, Mug? What did you say?"

"One day you and I were resting on this very beach," the coffee mug volunteers. "You were sad and reflective, having just returned from Ted's funeral. There was a darkness surrounding you. I remember the tuna fish sandwich, like the one you have now, sat untouched."

"Yes, that day is vivid in my mind. The sun was shining bright, much like today but, you are right, there was no light inside me." I pause, then whisper to myself, "still isn't."

Silence follows. Then I say, "I'm getting hungry, I think I am going to eat a little."

"Wait, don't eat yet," says Mug. "Here comes Raven hopping by. Let's talk with him."

"What seems to be the problem with you two?" inquires the Raven. "So forlorn you both look."

"My best friend died, and I am thinking about him. I still haven't come to terms with his death."

"Caw. Yes. I have some thoughts I would like to share with you about that, but unfortunately I am so hungry I am not thinking straight. Perhaps your tuna fish sandwich will provide me with the needed stamina I require to help you." Raven jumps up on the table and without approval begins to devour my sandwich.

Mug laughs. "You were hungry but hadn't eaten and now Raven is so smart that he's eating his fill while you sit and watch."

I stare at Mug, disgruntled and take a swig of coffee from him.

"Okay, Raven. You ate my sandwich, now help me."

"To be honest, it is not that easy," caws Raven. "First I must rest here on the beach and digest the wonderful tuna fish. And you are so cold and dark inside that I cannot help you when I am sleepy from eating so much."

Raven waddles over to the best lounge chair on the beach while its former occupant plays in the water. He spreads out the blanket left on the chair, takes a deep breath, sighs loudly, plops himself down, and soon begins to snore. With his stomach full of my food, he remains motionless.

A great gust of wind wakens Raven. Raven is lifted upon the wind and in a matter of seconds glides out of sight. The last thing I hear is, "Caw. I will return with help. Trust me."

The wind carries him higher and higher until he reaches the sun he had placed in the darkness many eons ago. Raven opens the pouch he always carries with him, plucks off a piece of the sun, places it in the pouch, and closes the opening. This has happened many times before. The sun is always willing to share himself with Raven because Raven released him from a box and the sun is forever grateful.

The great bird spreads his wings and the wind returns him to earth, in fact to the very beach where this adventure started. I watch Raven with curiosity as he ignores me and eats huckleberries left on a table. He settles down on the lounge chair he left earlier and once again drifts off to sleep.

Raven thinks of all the things he has in his pouch: a rock from a mountain nearby, a feather from his friend Eagle, a piece of white fish, and now part of the sun. "I am so lucky to have such a 'bundle' in my sacred pouch." He smiles and once again drifts off to sleep.

The sun begins to sink into the mountains on the other side of the lake. Raven stretches, shakes his dark feathers that reveal a white sheen, tilts his head and looks at me. He bounces over to where I am sitting, looks me in the eyes, and says, "First give me some potato chips, than we will talk." I oblige.

Full once again, Raven begins, "You, my sort of friend, are choosing only to see the loss of Ted, creating darkness inside you. In your self-pity you have removed the light from your soul and there is only darkness remaining. This is not only boring and unbalanced, but inappropriate. It has been fifteen years.

I hung the sun, moon, and stars in the sky to balance the boring and inappropriate darkness of the world. In you there is no balance, only darkness. Close your eyes and take a deep breath." As I did this Raven, in a flash, removed the sun from the pouch and blew it into my mouth. I was filled with warmth. The old mug smiled knowingly and thinks, "Ted would like this."

The great bird says, "I have hanged the sun in your breast. It is your choice to balance it with the darkness that also deserves a place. You can remove the sun if you choose and return to your angry and self-centered sad ways. My hope is that the sun remains in you as it does in the sky, bringing light to darkness and balance to your life. Intermingle the light and the dark within you, and you will find comfort and wisdom to supplement the loss of Ted."

"I know what you are referring to," I say to Raven. "There are times when I am at peace with the loss of Ted and grateful he was part of my life."

"So you say, but the darkness dominates," says Raven. "It is time to recognize your oneness with the universe and not just write about it. Living with the Great Spirit, the Great Mystery, is much different than intellectualizing about it."

And so it happens. Raven's breath fills me with the sun's warmth. My wise old mug continues to smile. I believe I hear Mug's thoughts, "Things will be better now. You see, peace comes when you realize your oneness with the universe and all its powers. When you realize the center of the Universe is within you. The Great Spirit is within each of us. Yes, even me, your old overused mug."

Another wind sweeps across the beach, shifting the sand and catching Raven, who has spread his wings. As he glides into the woods, his familiar caw returns as if to say, "I wish you well."

I awake with a start. Was that real? It felt real, but there is my tuna fish sandwich, untouched. And yet… and yet…I have a peace inside that was not there earlier. Raven on the Wind has gifted me with inner light and warmth. My old and now sacred mug was my ally. I feel the loss of Ted, but peace is alive and well inside me.

"What just happened, Mug? You don't mind if I call you Mug do you?" The coffee mug refuses to talk. Still, I show the courtesy of filling him with hot coffee. There is a familiar whisper in my ear, "Thank you, I like the feel of hot coffee" he says.

"What?" I respond, hoping to hear from Mug now that I am wide awake.

Silence.

I listen to a kid crying because the huckleberries he had picked that morning were missing.

A few days after Raven's visit on the beach, I sit on my familiar deck, watch the sunrise over the lake of sparkling blue glass, and ask myself, "What drew me to Raven?" What is the common denominator that brings together world history, Native American folklore, the mandorla, Rick Bartow, shamanism, Edgar Allen Poe, and so many people like me?

The answer lies in the blending of the material and spiritual that is explored in traditions throughout history and exemplified in the Native Amercian Raven of myth, legend, and folktale.

LOSS OF TRADITION

In our contemporary society we rely on social media, filtered news, limited experience, and an onslaught of hedonistic pleasures to define our worldview. The never ending quest for more money, more activity, fills our lives. In such a world, interpreting my experience on the beach as "real" is as ridiculous as Poe's Raven talking, Raven placing the sun in the sky, or even being smart enough to steal red berries. Such mystical happenings are relegated to folktales, primitive religions, getting caught up in the shaman's drum, or other types of events that manipulate the brain. Once lived spiritual traditions are now relegated to an intellectual study in hopes of understanding a long gone primitive culture.

Native Americans face pressure to abandon the traditions of their fathers in the name of "progress" and becoming "civilized." They are told, "Your traditions aren't rational; dancing, chanting, and pipe smoking are primitive acts. You are naively innocent, and it is time you entered the real world. For God's sake, we all know Raven didn't create the world! None of what you believe is true."

In fact, the Native American traditional experience of reality is mythical and mystical, not naive. It is tradition based in a living earth, equal rapport with animals, pathways to the Great Spirit, and ceremonies and folklore uplifting the shared tradition of the tribes. Truth requires context, and Native American tradition is that context. It is that tradition, threatened as it is, that brings different groups together.

Spiritual traditions are easily lost in our contemporary society. Once Native Americans spoke with the trees, knew different messages in the wind, and dwelt in the protective power of the Great Spirit. In today's society a tree is removed for a parking lot, the wind is transformed into smog, and protection is found in financial security not the great the Great Spirit.

Can any spiritual tradition hold its value and worth in today's society? Does long-lived folklore cease to "be" in the now and become only a useful tool for the study of yesterday's culture? Did Edgar Allan Poe's Raven foreshadow the coming world with his spoken word, "Nevermore?" Do the Greek, Norse, Native American and other mythologies have any meaning that is relevant today? Does my morning on the beach with Mug and Raven hold any value besides being a cute story, a fantasy?

To address these questions, it is important to understand what is being lost. I will focus the questions on Native American tradition.

To begin, there is no word in any of the over 220 Native American languages that is equivalent to the English word "religion." As close as the Native American languages come to "religion" is the word "tradition." Religion implies one optional way to observe and interpret the world. Tradition for the Native American is how the world is, there is no alternative. Tradition is not separated from culture or society. Rather tradition is inherent in the essence of life and a person's relationships to the earth, animals and other people. Tradition is the only way of understanding the world. Tradition is rooted in spirituality.

SPIRITUAL FOUNDATIONS

Spirituality is central to Native American culture and individual self-image. Spirituality is expressed through ceremonial rites and the peoples' relationship to the earth and all living things.

There are a wide variety of traditions among the various tribes, formed through different environments and tribal histories. While the traditions of tribes throughout the nation vary, there are *some* traditions shared by all tribes.

Raven reveals three fundamental aspects of Native American tradition shared by all tribes and are the foundation of my own worldview:

First, Raven of Native American tradition understands **all that is, the physical and the mystical are part of One.** Tradition does not fragment life into separate compartments. Even something as material and solid as a rock is understood to have its own life and is included in the spiritual whole.

Native American beliefs are often described as pantheism. Pantheism is the belief that reality is identical with divinity, all things have in their essence the divine, and therefore the Great Spirit and the universe are one and the same.

There is another word that better describes the Native American belief. Panentheism is where all is in the Great Spirit, but the Great Spirit transcends it. The Great Spirit or Great Mystery interpenetrates the universe but also transcends the universe of time and space. The Great Mystery is the "stillness" visited by the shaman and his ally, Raven.

"As you know," the Lakota Sioux Jenny Leading Cloud says, "We Indians think of the earth and the whole universe as a never-ending circle, and in this circle man is just another animal. The buffalo and the coyote are our brothers; the birds, our kind—they are all relatives. We end our prayers with the words mitakuye oyasis—'all my relations'—and that includes everything that grows, crawls, runs, creeps, hops, and flies on this continent. White people see man as nature's master and conqueror, but Indians, who are close to nature, know better."[8]

The sacred is experienced in the folklore and rites shared by those who participate in them with sincerity. Rites and folklore bind the animal kingdom, humans, the earth and the Sacred together. This binding experience is expressed in art forms, both visual and audible, and incorporated in ritual as well as daily life.

Rich Bartow understood this. He reached deep into the Northwest Native American history and tradition and translated it into contemporary fine art. He drew from the mythic relationship between human and animal and revealed their common lineage and shared soul. The Bundled Ravens can guide each of us to interpret existing myths and legends, place them in conversation with our current circumstances, and come to know ourselves better. The hermeneutic of placing a myth or legend, told for generations, in conversation with our lives is a gift to understanding our place in the world. Bartow's fine art is an icon, a window, through which we can see and understand ourselves better. In understanding all as part of One, Bartow's art symbolically blends animal and human into a single being.

In Native American tradition animals are essential to the spiritual life of humans. They were created first and, depending on the myth, create or aid the Great Spirit in the creation of humans. Animals such as the Raven provide an essential role for shamans to communicate with the Great Spirit. Animals are not owned by humans but share with us the earth and the heavens. In the spiritual world of myth and legend, animals are often wiser than humans, providing guidance and insight. Earth, too, is part of the common Spirit, part of One. It is respected and honored, not used for personal gain and then discarded.

---

[8] American Indian Myths and Legends, by Richard Erdoes and Alfonso Ortiz, Pantheon Books, New York. 1984. p. 5

This truth has lost its way in today's society. The earth, overwhelmed by excessive use, is raped in the name of greed, masked as progress. Animal rights groups fight an uphill battle against allowing endangered species to vanish from the earth.

There is an ancient poem from the Chukchee tribe in Siberia:

Everything that is
is alive

On a steep river bank
there's a voice that speaks
I have seen the master of that voice
he bowed to me
I spoke with him
he answers all my questions
everything that is alive
Little grey bird
little blue breast
sings in a hollow bough
she calls her spirits dances
sings her shaman songs
woodpecker on a tree
that's his drum
he's got a drumming nose
and the tree shakes
cries out like a drum
when the axe bites its side

All these things answer
my call

everything that is
is alive

the lantern walks around
the walls of this house have tongues
even the bowl has its own true home
that hides asleep in their bags
were up talking all night
Antlers on the graves
rise and circle the mounds
while the dead themselves get up
and go visit the living ones

It is our challenge to remember, to know, we share the same spirit with the earth and all living things.

The **Second** traditional foundation Raven teaches is **consciousness outside time.** Consciousness is beyond time and space yet not separate from them. In our rational world we tend to deny the existence of other states of consciousness and awareness, or we set aside mystical experiences and pretend they didn't happen.

The myths and legends about Raven never speak to his origin or creation. Humans are created in a variety of ways and within time, but Raven has always been, no beginning, no end, outside time. Raven myths often begin with words such as, "Before time began…".

Our language is oriented to understanding time as past, present, and future. Being completely in the now ("Eternal Now" in Christian tradition) is difficult to grasp in our hectic goal-oriented lives. Linear time is where we look for our values. We are continually changing, wanting the past to be inferior to current time which, if we are successful, will be less than the future will be. What's the old folktale one-line joke that helps define our culture? "He who dies with the most toys wins."

Linear time makes it almost "impossible to identify with a center of permanence that alone can give meaning and direction to change."[9]

The eternal Raven understands this. The "outside of time" center binds us to All, rejecting the contemporary experience of alienation from nature, the earth, and even other people.

Rites and ceremonies celebrate the mystical not the mundane. Spiritual life found in ritual folklore is celebrated in music, art, drama, and the shared word. Change takes place and is meaningful when it is related to the changeless. The "Changeless" was before time and informs the ever changing present. Raven on the wind is the mythical tie between the finite and the eternal. The eternal center is the ultimate mystery, the "Mystery" within and beyond all of us. All is sacred, and creation is respected and treated as such.

---

[9] The Spiritual Legacy of the American Indian by Joseph Brown (Commermorative Edition), World Wisdom, Inc. 2007. p. 87

The Blackfoot tell of gathering the skins of water animals such as ducks and kingfishers and making the skins, which represent sacred water power, into bags called "medicine bundles." The bags made of animal skins were gifted by their animal brothers and sisters. In the bags they placed the sweet weed nawak'osis. This sacred tobacco weed was smoked, with the rising smoke establishing a bridge to the sacred. Smoke carried upward on the wind was called "holy smoke." Oneness with the animals brings them to the smoke ceremony that takes them to the Great Beyond where time is not.

The truth of consciousness beyond time is expressed in detail in the Lakota Sioux legend of the White Buffalo Woman and the Sacred Pipe. This is arguably the most important and central legend of the Lakota Sioux.

The Sioux were a warrior tribe where "woman shall not walk before man." Yet, in this central Sioux legend it is the mythical woman, White Buffalo Woman, who is dominant and the savior of the people.

"Early one morning the chief sent two of his young men to hunt for game. They went on foot, because at that time the Sioux didn't yet have horses. They searched everywhere but could find nothing….(Then) they saw something coming toward them from far off, but the figure was floating instead of walking. From this they knew that the person was wakan, holy, not of time.

As it came nearer, they realized that it was a beautiful young woman, more beautiful than any they had ever seen, with two round, red dots of face paint on her cheeks. She wore a wonderful white buckskin outfit, tanned until it shone a long way in the sun. It was embroidered with sacred and marvelous designs of porcupine quill, in radiant colors no ordinary woman could have made. This Wakan stranger was Ptesan-Wi, White Buffalo Woman.

One young man desired her body and stretched out his hand to touch her….Lightning instantly struck the young man and burned him up.

To the other scout who had behaved with respect, the White Buffalo Woman said: 'Good things I am bringing, something holy to your nation. Go back to the camp and tell the people to prepare for my arrival.'

So the people put up the big medicine tipi and waited. After four days they saw White Buffalo Woman approaching, carrying her bundle before her….The chief addressed her respectfully, saying: 'Sister, we are glad you have come to instruct us.'

The white buffalo was and is the most sacred of animals to the Sioux. When the mythical white robed figure met with the Sioux chief she opened the bundle revealing the chanunpa, the sacred pipe. She grasped the stem with her right hand and the bowl with her left, and thus the pipe has been held ever since.

White Buffalo Woman explained how the pipe was to be used. She filled the pipe with willow-bark tobacco and lit the 'fire without end,' a flame to be passed on from generation to generation. 'With the holy pipe,' she said, 'you will walk like a living prayer with your feet resting upon the earth and the pipe stem reaching into the sky. When you walk with the sacred pipe your body forms a living bridge between the Sacred Beneath and the Sacred Above.'

'Look at the Bowl,' she continued. 'Its stone represents the flesh and blood of the red man.' White Buffalo Woman paused then her legendary words continued, 'The buffalo represents the universe and its four directions, because he stands on four legs, for the four ages of creation. The buffalo was put in the west by Wakan Tanka (Great Spirit/Great Mystery) at the making of the world, to hold back the waters. Each year he loses one hair, and in every one of the four ages he loses a leg. The sacred hoop will end when all the hair and legs of the great buffalo are gone, and the water comes back to cover the earth.

The wooden stem of the chanupa stands for all that grows on the earth. Twelve feathers hanging from where the stem—the skull—are from Wanblee Galeshka, the spotted eagle (note: equivalent to Raven in Northwest Mythology), the very sacred bird who is the Great Spirit's messenger and the wisest of all flying ones. You are joined to all things in the universe, for they all cry out to Tunkashila (Sacred Grandfather). Look at the bowl: engraved in it are seven circles of various sizes. They stand for the seven sacred ceremonies you will practice with this pipe, and for the Ocheti Shakowin, the seven sacred campfires of our Lakota nation.'"

White Buffalo Woman came from outside time to provided understanding and meaning to the linear changing events in time and within and outside the tribe. Linear events found meaning when they were related to the eternal Great Spirit/Great Mystery outside of time.

As with White Buffalo Woman, in Northwest myths and legends Raven was and remains the mediator between the Great Above and the Great Beneath. The pipe ceremony is still used to bring forth the relationship between the two worlds. Every teepee and sweat lodge has a fire ring in its center and a hole in the top of the sweat lodge or teepee where the smoke escapes to the heavens. The smoke is the pathway to and from the Great Spirit.

The Raven, for many shamans, is the ally flowing with the shaman on the wind of the "holy smoke," the messenger and mediator between the Great Above (Spirit/Mystery) and the Great Beneath (life of humans, animals, earth). The Great Above is outside time and when called upon informs and heals the life's experience in the world of time.

When warring tribes would seek peace, they came together bringing separate pieces of the pipe. One tribe would provide the sacred bowl, another tribe the sacred stem, and the third would bring spiritual tobacco. If only two tribes met they would mix the tobacco each had produced. The pipe pieces would be assembled showing the common spiritual base the tribes shared. The pipe would be smoked creating holy smoke going to the Great Above. Understanding their common mystical heritage, the leaders of the tribes would begin peace talks. Therefore, peace talks always began with the recognition of the sacred, their commonality in sharing the Great Spirit that is outside time and space.

When we lose our common foundation, our shared life with all that is living, it is essential to restore it, or peace becomes illusive. Without a common foundation the "other" is demonized. There is only black and white, right and wrong, no mandorla. Compromise becomes weakness rather than strength.

The usury of other people, dehumanizing of those we do not agree with, and believing if something isn't to my personal advantage "forget it", can lead us to ignore or reject our common heritage. In such a narcissistic self-centered world there is no pipe to put together, no blending of the white and black Raven, no understanding of a common source to draw on, and nothing outside time and space. There is only self-interest, regardless the cost.

The Sacred Pipe and the sound of the Raven's "caw" are to remind us we that share a common unchanging spiritual base, the Great Spirit/Mystery that informs and guides our lives on the living earth. Our strength is in our oneness where we find healing for our separation and meaning in our unity.

The **third** Native American tradition informed by Raven is the **sacredness of wind or breath.**

Webster's definition of "spirit" is personified in the Raven. Webster defines "spirit" as "breathing or wind, related to." Raven is both spiritual and material. He comes from the Spirit World and lives in the physical world. He is used by shamans to take them on the wind into the world of the Great Spirit. Raven is carried on the wind and without it cannot fly.

The word "breath" comes from the Latin 'spiritus', which means "that which gives life or vitality to a system" (human, social, organizational). The vitality of the 'spiritus' becomes part of us and yet is greater than us. Such an understanding is fundamental to Native American tradition.

When we breathe, we take in breath and it gives us life. The invisible becomes the life-giver to the visible body. Some unseen breath remains within us when we exhale. Breath is the source of all life and is greater than individual life.

When we exhale, our breath is external to ourselves and is part of the universal breath. When we understand that our breath is shared with others, when we realize we are sharing the same breath, we then understand that we share life with all. Trees, plants, fish, animals, and people rely on shared breath for life. The Spirit Wind brings and sustains life for us individually and collectively.

The great Jewish theologian, Martin Buber, in his classic 1957 book, I and Thou, recognized that we are less than we can be when we only care about our own life. He believed human value comes from unity, oneness. He recognized the *spiritus* within all, breath bringing unity.

Unity with others takes us from an I-It (separated) relationship where the other is only a thing, to the unity of I-Thou (Oneness). Buber described God as within the I-Thou. He had trouble with the actual word "God" because it had been used and misused in so many ways that it was impossible to come up with a universally accepted definition. Buber contended that "I-Thou" is a definition of the Universal Spirit in all our life and could be embraced by every religion. He had a premise that "All real living is meeting."

Hence, in an I-Thou relationship, the other is not an It, as the one Indian scout made White Buffalo Woman and was destroyed by doing so. True rapport does not have objects. I-Thou becomes a spiritual union of two. We are isolated and alone in the world when we see ourselves as separate from everything else.

Buber opened his world to mythology, mysticism, and Native American tradition when he added I-Thou relationships are not limited to people but can be experienced by all living things. Rapport goes both ways from person to animal and from animal and person to the earth. He was well known for his description of a person's I-Thou relationship with a tree, where both recognize the common Spirit in each other.

The spiritual quality of breath or wind is manifest in our speech. Without breath or wind there is no sound. And words have a force that is integral to the specific sounds. Words come from non-physical thought and are born in breath. Through breath Stillness becomes word. Words are sacred and must be used with care. This is especially true when used in a ceremonial context or in sharing a story, legend or myth. A creation story, for example, is more than just a story. In the world of myth, every time a creation story is told, it is a re-enactment of the creation itself. Breath, Spirit comes forth in the spoken word. The myth is not bound by time and space.

Breath or wind without interruption has no sound, it just is. The name "Yahweh" ("Lord' in Hebrew scripture) originally had no vowels and was impossible to speak. The spiritual mystery, brought forth from the Hebrew "Silent Awe," was silent and still as air without interruption. The Great Spirit of Native American tradition, as Yahweh, originally had no spoken sound. The Great Spirit/Mystery just is, not spoken.

While many shamans may not be familiar with the Latin word *spiritus,* they certainly understand the meaning behind the word. Wind is Spirit. In a sacred pipe ceremony, The Sioux leader Black Elk addresses the great universal Spirit of the Sioux, *Wakan-Tanka*: "O You who control the sacred winds, and who live there where we always face, Your breath gives life, and it is from You and to You that our generations come and go."[10]

In Genesis 8:1-3 the wind brings renewed life following the life destroying flood: "And God made a wind blow over the earth, and the waters subsided; the fountains of the deep and the windows of the heavens were closed, the rain from the heavens were restrained, and the waters receded from the earth continually."

There is an old Tlingit legend that goes like this: "Now Raven went off to a certain place and created West Wind. Raven said, "No matter how hard you blow you will hurt no one. You are good and bring breath to life.

Resting on my beloved McCall beach, sipping coffee on this beautiful September day, I think back to the story of the black and white raven brothers and how one slew the other. Truth, balance, and self-understanding took place with the blending of the two brothers. For me balance is found in the quiet of the mountains, and experiencing the Great Spirit entwined with the material world in the Great Beneath, allowing me to face myself

---

[10] The Sacred Pipe by Joseph Brown, University of Oklahoma Press. 1953. (chapter IV Crying for a Vision, loc. 773)

honestly and learn from my paradoxes. The Great Above touching the earth, creating a sacred time of quiet, of solitude, of silence and stillness, challenges me to ever see myself anew.

I reflect on the Red and Blue Raven Bundles. I no longer analyze the art, rather, I experience it. It takes me through a wide range of emotions—feeling the creative power inherent in the universe, the destructions in our lives and the rebirth to new understandings, and the realization life tricks and deceives us all from time to time. Life is not to be trusted, just loved and lived.

Native American myths, legends, and folktales of Raven demand personal attention. Rick Bartow's artistic messages cry to be experienced and interpreted. The shaman for centuries has taken to the wind with his ally Raven on flight to the Great Spirit, gained knowledge and healing power, returned to heal the mind, body, and spirit of the earth, the tribe, and individuals. My hope is that Edgar Allan Poe, who was broken by life, has found the eternal he speaks of in his last book, Eureka.

The Sun has returned to its resting place behind the mountain. Night is swallowing the lake beach. A cool wind blows over the land that is part of me and I of it. I take a deep breath, giving thanks for all that is. In the woods behind me I hear the silence broken by the challenging and reassuring ancient sound, "caw." Raven on the eternal wind.

ACKNOWLEDGEMENTS

This book was written in part and inspirited by individuals I never knew and are no longer with us. I thank Rick Bartow, Edgar Allan Poe, centuries old raven stories from around the world, and the enduring raven folklore of Native American tradition. All were essential for this book to be written.

Charles Froelick, owner of the Froelick Gallary in Portland, Oregon, provided unique insights into the life of Rick Bartow and was instrumental in securing the use of Bartow's art for this book.

Editor, Ruth Karpen, made countless edits and challenged me to incorporate more of my personal experience into the book. Significant editing and insight was provided by Jonna Hansmeier, Mary Mossay, and Sheri Cheung. Jon Turk approved the sharing of his amazing adventure and provided clarity to my understanding of the Siberian shaman, Moolynaut. Rex Reddick from Crazy Crow Trading Post provided encouragement and the use of his artwork. The book benefited from the encouragement of *The Questers* of Boise, Idaho, and countless conversations with friends and family. My wife, Joy, painted the book's cover, the mandorla, and the small raven at the beginning of each chapter. She made edits to my writing, and provided time and encouragement to me every step of the way. This book would not have been written without her support.

BIBLIOGRAPHY

A variety of books, reports, and interviews were used to create this book. The information was supplemented by my academic degrees in theology and a lifelong interest Native American tradition and mythology. Folklore in the form of myths, legends, and folktales is created by unknown authors and found in oral traditions around the globe. No original sources or authors are acknowledged because they do not exist. I have acknowledged sources where specific stories have been found. New folktales that are sighted in this writing are available to the general public through social media. Countless books and social media provide avenues to many ancient myths, legends, and folktales as well.

The following references the specific sources used in this book.

OPENING POEMS:

RavenWind and *Wings on the Wind* by Hartzell Cobbs

INTRODUCTION:

Bronner, Simon
2017 Folklore: The Basics. Routledge, New York.

Dundes, Alan
2007 Meaning of Folklore. Utah State University Press.

Dundes, Alan
1991 Never Try to Teach a Pig to Sing. Wayne State University Press.

McNeill, Lynne S.
2013 Folklore Rules: A Fun Quick and Useful Introduction. Utah State University Press.

CHAPTER ONE:

de Lint, Charles
2017 The Wind in His Heart. Triskell Press, Ottawa, ON, Canada.

Feher-Elston, Catherine
1991 Ravensong. Northland Publishing, Flagstaff, Arizona.

Gaiman, Neil
2017 Norse Mythology. W.W. Norton & Company. New York.

Jennings, Peter
2017 A Cacophony of Corvids. Gruff Books, Halstead Essex.

Hemmingway, Ernest
1929 A Farewell to Arms. Charles Scribner's Sons, New York.

Johnson, Robert
2013 Owning Your Own Shadow. HarperCollins Publisher, Sydney, Australia.

Irwin, Louis Two Ravens,
1996 Two Ravens: The Life and Teaching of a Spiritual Warrior. Destiny Books, Rochester, Vermont.

CHAPTER THREE:

Dembicki, Matt (compiled by)
2010 Trickster: Native American Tales, a Graphic Collection. Fulcrum, Colorado

Edwards, Gavin
2016 The Tao of Bill Murray. Random House, New York.

Erdoes, Richard
1984 American Indian Trickster Tales (Myths and Legends). Random House, Canada.

Hyde, Lewis
1998 Trickster Makes the World. Farrar, Straus and Giroux, New York.

Radin, Paul
2015 The Trickster: A Study in American Indian Mythology. Pickle Partners Publishing. (originally published in 1956)

CHAPTER FOUR:

Bartow, Rick
2002 My Eye. University of Washington Press. p. 15.

Bartow, Rick
2015 Things You Know but Cannot Explain. University of Oregon Press.

CHAPTER FIVE:

Grim, John
1983 *The Shaman.* University of Oklahoma Press.

Harner, Michael
1980 The Way of the Shaman. HarperCollins Publishing.

Turk, Jon
2010 The Raven's Gift. Macmillan-Macmillan Publishers, London, England.

Porta, Giovannita Battista
1558 Natural Magick

CHAPTER SIX:

Collins, Paul
2014 Edgar Allan Poe: The Fever Called Living. Amazon Publishing, New York.

Meyers, Jeffrey
1992 Edgar Allan Poe: his Life and Legacy. Rowman & Littlefield Publishing Group, New York.

Poe, Edgar Allan
2017 Edgar Allan Poe: The Complete Tales and Poems. Book House Publishing.

CHAPTER SEVEN:

Brown, Joseph
1953 The Sacred Pipe. University of Oklahoma Press.

Brown, Joseph
2007 The Spiritual Legacy of the American Indian. *(Commemorative Edition).* World Wisdom, Inc.

Buber, Martin
1957 I and Thou *(second edition).* Scribner Publishing, New York.

Erodoes, Richard and Ortiz, Alfonso
1984 American Indian Myths and Legends. Pantheon Books, New York.

Leo Tolstoy's Diary, 1910

The written words of Rick Bartow are taken from interviews he had with Charles Froelick. Rick Bartow's art is presented by courtesy of the Froelick Gallery in Portland, Oregon.

"The Jon Turk Story" is presented with permission from and edits by Jon Turk.

All artwork in the book is used with permission or is in the public domain.

Printed in the United States
By Bookmasters